JITNEY

JITNEY

August Wilson

THE OVERLOOK PRESS
WOODSTOCK & NEW YORK

First published in the United States in 2001 by
The Overlook Press, Peter Mayer Publishers, Inc.
Woodstock & New York

WOODSTOCK:
One Overlook Drive
Woodstock, NY 12498
www.overlookpress.com
[for individual orders, bulk and special sales, contact our Woodstock office]

NEW YORK:
141 Wooster Street
New York, NY 10012

Library of Congress Cataloging-in-Publication Data

Wilson, August.
Jitney / August Wilson.—1st ed.
p. cm.
1. Hill District (Pittsburgh, Pa.)—Drama. 2. African American neighborhoods—
Drama. 3. African Americans—Drama. 4. Pittsburgh (Pa.)—Drama.
5. Taxicab drivers—Drama. I. Title
PS35 73.I45677 J58 2001   812'.54—dc21   2001033962

Book design and type formatting by Bernard Schleifer
Manufactured in the United States of America
FIRST EDITION
1 3 5 7 9 8 6 4 2
ISBN 1-58567-186-X

For Azula Carmen Wilson
who burst upon the world clothed in the light of angelic grace.

You are more blessing than I deserve.

INTRODUCTION

Marion Isaac McClinton

People love August Wilson's *Jitney*. This is not some theory that is open to a panel debate. It is a simple statement of fact. Everywhere I go where *Jitney* has gone before, if I am wearing my *Jitney* jacket or signature Borsalino hat, I am stopped by people and told at great length with a greater outpouring of deep, honest emotion how they loved the play and how genuinely touched and profoundly moved they were by it. How they came back time and again, bringing family and friends along with them, how it did not matter if they were black, white or Martian, that they were not watching a play—they were watching their own lives acted out before their very eyes. People wanted to know whatever there was to know about *Jitney*. "Are you going to do it again?" "Where is *Jitney* going next?" "Where did you find such a great cast?" "Were they really *Jitney* drivers?" One time there was even a man who wanted to know if August Wilson planned to write a sequel to *Jitney*, as if it were a Hollywood franchise, like *Star Wars* or *Indiana Jones*.

But the most peculiar and moving moment was my being stopped by a man in St. Paul, Minnesota, at the bank, when I was in a hurry and frankly in no mood to talk. He stopped me and said, point blank, "You don't know nothing about a jitney?" Not "What do you know about a jitney?" but "You don't know nothing about a jitney!" Obviously, he must have thought I bought my jacket at Sears. I was about to tell him everything I knew about a jitney, and a few more things that weren't on his list of things to learn but were on mine to teach, when he told me he had put himself through high school *and* college driving jitneys, that his father drove jitneys for over thirty years and had raised *two* families off that money. He was from Omaha and he was in a mood where he wanted to talk. There was something he wanted to say, and there was something he wanted to know. He wanted to tell me how he came to St. Paul, how he hadn't planned on coming here but wasn't planning on staying in Omaha either. How he got to St. Paul and found out there weren't any jitneys to drive, so he did all other kinds of work but felt something was wrong. The work didn't sit right with him. Something was wrong. Then he told me it hit him plain as day, right between the eyes. When he was driving jitneys in Omaha, he wasn't just making money to take care of himself, he was also doing something to help take care of his community. He was, as Becker says in the play, "providing a service." It made him feel better about himself and his place in the world. It made him feel like his feet could fill out his daddy's shoes. It gave him not just a purpose but a direction in life: to serve his community. So he went and enrolled at the police academy, became a cop, even started a boxing program for kids in the neighborhood. We also found out, when he told me his name, that he had jailed me once (a misunderstanding that got understood), and he told me how proud he was to see how I turned out. But then he asked me a question, something he wanted to know, and it will stick with me forever. *Jitney,* which he saw at Penumbra Theatre in St. Paul, (in a production I didn't direct) wasn't just our story, he said, "It *is* who we are. It's not our *story,* it's our truth, the facts of the matter concerning our life in the land of the free and home of the brave. You know what I'm saying?" He was concerned if it wasn't coming back, "Who is going to tell it? Who is going to tell the story so that we can feel it? That's important, man, because once you feel it, then it's *yours.*" I assured him that the story would not be lost, that *Jitney* was being published, and that the story would continue to be told. He felt relieved and asked if I could get him a copy when it came out. I told him I would, and we talked for a few minutes more, then went our separate ways. Separate but very connected. Then it hit me, hit me like a shout in the night. August Wilson's *Jitney,* just like the rest of his canon, is much too important to be left solely to the whimsy of memory. It must be written and passed down like the Ten Commandments: The story of Becker and Booster, a tale of a father and son, becomes the legend of every parent and child. The story of Youngblood and Rena, two young adults attempting with determination to do the heavy lifting that true love calls for, while also trying to make a decent and better life for their son. Turnbo, Doub, Fielding, Shealy, and Philmore, the drivers and customers of the jitney station, men who meet each day straight up and head on and who only want to reach the end of the day with the same amount of dignity and integrity that they began with. These are the stories that must be told and passed on because they reveal to us our humanity, giving us the hope that we might walk our day with a similar grace and nobility.

August Wilson is the griot, our Homer, our Shakespeare, our grandfather sitting on the front porch telling us the stories that we need to know. We need these stories. They matter. They mean so much to so many different people. They're honest and they say "This here is our place," a place that is inherited, just like our blood and bones, a place where stories live that help to define who we have been and who we are, so we might wonder at the possibilities of who we can be. This is our place to stand upon, so that we can snatch the future and claim it forever, never to lose it again.

These are the things August Wilson wants you to know. August Wilson is a master jitney driver. It is how he protects and serves. He gives us rides to all the places we need to get to, return trip included at no extra fee. He will not leave you someplace without a way back home, and he will make sure you have more coming back than what you left with. I can guarantee you that. I ain't alone, either. People love August Wilson's *Jitney.* If you don't know, you better ask somebody.

CHARACTERS

YOUNGBLOOD, jitney driver and Vietnam veteran—mid-late twenties

TURNBO, jitney driver who is always interested in the business of others

FIELDING, jitney driver and former tailor, with a dependency on alcohol

DOUB, longtine jitney driver and Korean War veteran

SHEALY, numbers taker who often uses the jitney station as his base

PHILMORE, local hotel doorman, recurring jitney passenger

BECKER, well-respected man who runs the jitney station—in his sixties

BOOSTER, Becker's son, recently released from prison—in his early 40's

RENA, Youngblood's girlfriend and mother of their young son

Jitney had its world premiere at the Allegheny Repertory Theater in Pittsburgh, Pennsylvania, in October 1982. It was then presented by the Penumbra Theatre in St. Paul, Minnesota in 1985. Subsequent productions of a revised version of Jitney were performed at the following theaters: Pittsburgh Public Theater, Pittsburgh, Pennsylvania, June 1996; Crossroads Theater, New Brunswick, New Jersey, April 1997; Huntington Theatre, Boston, Massachusetts, October 1998; Center Stage, Baltimore, Maryland, January 1999; Studio Arena, Buffalo, New York, March 1999; GeVa Theatre, Rochester, New York, April 1999; Goodman Theatre, Chicago, Illinois, June 1999; Mark Taper Forum, Los Angeles, California, January 2000.

Jitney had its New York premiere at the Second Stage Theatre on April 25, 2000, with the following cast:

YOUNGBLOOD	Russell Hornsby
TURNBO	Stephen McKinley Henderson
FIELDING	Anthony Chisholm
DOUB	Barry Shabaka Henley
SHEALY	Willis Burks II
PHILMORE	Leo V. Finnie III
BECKER	Paul Butler
RENA	Michole Briana White
BOOSTER	Carl Lumbly

Director: Marion McClinton
Set Design: David Gallo
Costume Design: Susan Hilferty
Lighting Design: Donald Holder
Sound Design: Rob Milburn
Production Stage Manager: Narda Alcorn

ACT ONE

SCENE 1

(The time is early fall, 1977. The setting is a gypsy cab station in Pittsburgh, Pennsylvania. The paint is peeling off the walls, and the floor is covered with linoleum that is worn through in several areas. In the middle of the wall stage left sits an old-fashioned pot-bellied stove that dominates the room. Upstage of it is a blackboard on which is written the rates to different parts of the city, and the daily, marginally illegal policy numbers. Next to the blackboard a sign reads "Beckers's
R   u   l   e   s   :
1. No overcharging; 2. Keep car clean; 3. No drinking; 4. Be courteous; 5. Replace and clean tools." Downstage on the wall is a pay telephone. The entire right wall is made up of the entrance down right and a huge picture window. Along the upstage wall is a sofa, with several chairs of various styles and ages scattered about to complete the setting.

As the scene opens it is mid-morning. YOUNGBLOOD *and* TURNBO *sit facing each other on folding chairs in front of the sofa. They are playing checkers, with the checkerboard on their knees in front of them.* FIELDING *sits in a chair down left.)*

YOUNGBLOOD (*agitated*)
Naw! You can't do that! How you gonna take my man?

TURNBO
I'm gonna jump him, fool!

YOUNGBLOOD
How you gonna jump him with the man sitting there! I got a man sitting there! Is you blind?

TURNBO

Well put him where he belongs then! I ain't seen him sitting there. I thought he was on the other square.
(He studies the board and makes his move.
YOUNGBLOOD *jumps his man.)*

YOUNGBLOOD

Don't you know I was the checker champ of 'Nam.

TURNBO

Boy, ain't nobody studying you. (*He moves.*) There! Champ that!
*(*FIELDING *eases a half-pint bottle of gin from under the cushion of the chair. Discovering it is empty, he eases it back.)*

YOUNGBLOOD (*studying the board*)

I done told you who you playing with now. Can't nobody beat me. I'm like Muhammad Ali. I'm the greatest!

FIELDING (*gets up suddenly*)

Youngblood, let me have four dollars. I got to go.

TURNBO (*does a double jump*)

Come on and move, checker champ! What's the matter now? Huh?

YOUNGBLOOD

I ain't got it, Fielding. If I had it you know I'd give it to you.

TURNBO

Come on and play. Checker Champ.

FIELDING

Turnbo, let me have four dollars.

TURNBO (*to* YOUNGBLOOD, *agitated*)

Will you come on and move, man!

FIELDING

Let me have the four dollars.

TURNBO

Fielding, you know better than to ask me for anything.

*(*YOUNGBLOOD *moves, and* TURNBO *jumps two of his men.)*

King me! King me! Come on, Checker Champ, let me beat you again.

(The phone rings.)

YOUNGBLOOD

No, you cheat old man.

*(*FIELDING *answers the phone.)*

FIELDING

Car service. (*pause*) East Liberty? Whereabouts in East Liberty? (*pause*) That'll be four dollars. (*pause*) Lady, I don't care what nobody else charge you that's a four dollar trip. (*pause*) All right. Green car. What's the address again? (*pause*) I'll be right there.

(He hangs up as DOUB *enters.)*

FIELDING

Doub, let me have four dollars.

DOUB

What?

FIELDING

I got to make a run to East Liberty. Give me four dollars, I'll give it back to you.

DOUB

Hell, nigger, I ain't no bank.

FIELDING

Aw, give me the four dollars. I got to get some gas.

TURNBO

If you don't go out and drink up your money you'd have four dollars and wouldn't have to be asking nobody.

FIELDING

Ain't nobody ask you what I do with my money.

(to DOUB*)*

Let me have the four dollars, I'll give it back to you.

DOUB (*going into his pocket*)

Here . . . here . . . don't ask me for nothing else. This is
your one time in life to ask me for something.

(He hands him the money.)

You bring my four dollars back here too.

(FIELDING exits.)

TURNBO

Fielding ain't gonna do nothing but drink up that money.
He going right out there to the State Store.

(The phone rings. YOUNGBLOOD answers it.)

YOUNGBLOOD

Car service. (*pause*) Giant Eagle? Wait a minute, you gotta
get somebody else.

TURNBO

Here . . . I'll take it.

(He takes the phone.)

Yeah? Which Giant Eagle? (*pause*) All right. Be right
there. Brown car. You already checked out and ready to go
cause I ain't gonna be waiting. (*pause*) Okay.

(TURNBO exits. DOUB watches YOUNGBLOOD.)

YOUNGBLOOD

What you looking at me for?

DOUB

I ain't said nothing to you.

YOUNGBLOOD

I ain't gonna mess up my car hauling people's groceries
around.

DOUB

What you telling me for? I don't care about your business.
Becker's the one you ought to be telling what you is and
ain't gonna do.

(SHEALY enters.)

SHEALY

How's everybody in here?

YOUNGBLOOD

Hey Shealy.

DOUB

I see your boy down the street got a brand new car.

YOUNGBLOOD

Who? Who got a new car?

DOUB

Pope who own that restaurant down on Centre.

YOUNGBLOOD

What'd he get?

DOUB

He got a brand new shiny Buick Riviera. How much did he hit for, Shealy?

SHEALY

You know me, Doub. I don't be putting nobody's business in the street. First thing you know somebody be done got killed talking about "Shealy said . . . " I ain't gonna have that on my conscience. I don't know nothing.

DOUB

I know he hit big. He been playing that 261 every day for years.

SHEALY

I don't know nothing about it . . . but I do know he's closing up his restaurant. The city's tearing it down.

DOUB

They gonna tear it down before it fall down.

YOUNGBLOOD

I didn't know you and Pope was tight.

SHEALY

We ain't tight. I don't know why Doub wanna tie me up with him.

DOUB

Oh now . . . I remember when you all used to be tight.

SHEALY

Must be when he had that little yellow gal working for
him. That's the only time you ever see me down there.

DOUB

What ever happened to that gal?

SHEALY

She married to one of them boys that drive a bus. That's
what I hear.

DOUB

She wasn't the one, huh?

SHEALY

Naw she wasn't the one. I thought she was but then I believe
Rosie done put a curse on me. She don't want me to have
no other woman. But then she didn't want me. I told her
baby, just tell me what kind of biscuits you want to make.
I'm like the mill-man I can grind it up any way you want.
She knew I was telling the truth too. She couldn't say nothing about that. She say you a poor man. What I need with a
poor man? I told her say if I make a hundred I'll give you
ninety-nine. She didn't trust me on that one but I went down
to the crap game, hit six quick licks, left with a hundred and
sixty-three dollars. I went on back up there. She let me in. I
lay   a
hundred dollars down on the table and told her, "Now, if I
can just get one of them back I'd be satisfied." She reached
down and handed me a dollar and I went on in the room
and went to bed. Got up and she had my breakfast on the
table. It wasn't soon long that ninety-nine dollars ran out
and next thing I knew she had barred the door. I went on
and left but I never could get her off my mind. I said I was
gonna find me another woman. But every time I get hold to
one . . . time I lay down with them . . . I see Rosie's face. I
told myself the first time I lay down with a woman and don't
see her face then that be the one I'm gonna marry. That be
my little test. Now with that little yellow gal used to work
down at Pope's I seen Rosie's face . . . but it was blurry. Like
a cloud or something come over it. I say, "I got to try this
again. Maybe next time I won't see nothing."
    She told me she didn't want to see me no more. She told

me come back same time tomorrow and if she changed her mind she'd leave the key in the mailbox. I went up there and there was one man in the house and two others sitting on the doorstep. I don't know who had the key.
(The phone rings. YOUNGBLOOD *answers it.)*

YOUNGBLOOD
Car service. *(pause)* Yeah. Shealy.
*(*SHEALY *takes the phone.)*

SHEALY
Shealy here.
(He takes out a pad and pencil and begins writing.)

YOUNGBLOOD
I'm going next door to Clifford's.
*(*YOUNGBLOOD *exits.)*

SHEALY *(into phone)*
Six seventy-one straight. Four sixty-nine boxed for a dollar. I got it. I'll see you down Irv's later on.
(He hangs up the phone.)
You ain't seen Becker have you?

DOUB
He was by here earlier this morning. I think he had to make a run to take care of some business.

SHEALY
You know his boy getting out of the penitentiary next month.
(The phone rings. DOUB *crosses to the phone.)*

DOUB
No kidding.

SHEALY
After all them years.

DOUB
Time go along and it come around.

SHEALY
It don't never stop.

DOUB (*into phone*)
Car service. (*pause*) Where? (*pause*) Be right there. Blue car.
(DOUB *hangs up the phone.*)

DOUB

Shealy give me a dollar on that six seventy-four, I'll give
it to you when I get back.
(DOUB *exits.* SHEALY *sits in a chair and goes
over his number slips.* PHILMORE *enters.*)

SHEALY

Hey, Philmore.

PHILMORE

Ain't no cars here?

SHEALY

Doub just left . . . he be back in a minute.

PHILMORE

I got to get home. I been out all night and half the morning. My old lady gonna be mad at me.

SHEALY

You been out all night, huh?

PHILMORE

I went down the Working Men's Club. They had Kenny Fisher
down there. You couldn't hardly get in. I ain't never seen so
many people. You used to have to have a job to get in there.

SHEALY

I know they glad they changed that rule. Wouldn't nobody
be down there.

PHILMORE

I'd be down there. I got me a job.

SHEALY

I know. You work down the hotel. You been there a while.

PHILMORE

Six years. I been down there six years. Started May sixteen, nineteen seventy-one. Been down there six years and
ain't never missed a day. And I ain't never been late. I'm

supposed to get a raise. My old lady told me when I get my
raise she was gonna . . .
>   (YOUNGBLOOD *enters.*)

SHEALY

There go Youngblood.

PHILMORE

Come on, take me home. I got to get home. My old lady
gonna be mad at me.

YOUNGBLOOD

Where you live at?

PHILMORE

You know where I live at. Everybody know where I live
at. I live out there above the Frankstown Bar.

YOUNGBLOOD

That's a four dollar trip. You got four dollars?

PHILMORE

Look here . . . let me show you something. Watch this.
>   (*He builds a pyramid out of dollar bills, then
>   blows them over.*)

Now when my old lady tells me I been out blowing my
money . . . you can tell her it's the truth.

YOUNGBLOOD (*laughing*)

You see this, Shealy?

PHILMORE

Shealy done seen me do that before.

SHEALY

Go on, Philmore!
>   (YOUNGBLOOD *and* PHILMORE *exit. The phone
>   rings, and* SHEALY *answers it.*)

SHEALY

Yeah? (*pause*) Who? (*pause*) Naw, Mr. Becker ain't here.
Who? (*pause*) Let me see if I got this. Mr. Pease.
Pittsburgh Renewal Council. Yeah, I'll tell him.
>   (TURNBO *enters.*)

TURNBO

Boy, I don't know what this world's coming to. You know
McNeil don't you?

SHEALY

Who?

TURNBO

McNeil! McNeil what live up on Webster. Old Lady
McNeil, got them two boys and work cleaning up down at
the courthouse.

SHEALY (*trying to recognize the name*)

McNeil? I don't know . . .

TURNBO (*agitated*)

You know who I'm talking about! McNeil! Use to be
Brownie's old lady. You know Brownie was staying up
there trying to help her raise them two boys. One of them
got an old funny shaped head.

SHEALY

Oh, yeah. Yeah, I know who you talking about now.

TURNBO

Well, the boy come by here a little while ago this morning.
The oldest one, can't be no more than sixteen or seventeen at
the most. Come by here and asked me to carry him on a trip
to the Northside. Then he say he got to make a stop up on
Whiteside Road. I carried him up there and he go into one of
them houses and come on out carrying a television. He ain't said
nothing about no television now. I told him it was gonna cost
him two dollars more for me to be hauling around a television.
Had me carry him over on the Northside to the pawnshop.
    Now, I know the boy done stole the television, but I ain't
said nothing. I just want my money. Come on back and
stopped at Pat's Place to get me some tobacco, and the fellows standing around just happened to mention the name of
this woman who done had her television stolen. Don't you
know that boy done went and stole his grandmama's television! Name is Bolger. Miss Sarah Bolger. That's old lady
McNeil's mother. I used to carry her to church before she
got too old to go. Steal his own grandmother's television!

SHEALY

That ain't nothing, Turnbo. I seen worse than that.

(BECKER *enters.*)

TURNBO

Yeah, I have too. But what would make someone want to
steal their grandmama's television? I can't figure it out.
Becker, you know McNeil what live up on Webster used
to be Brownie's old lady . . . work cleaning up at the courthouse . . . got them two boys . . . one of them got an old
funny shaped head . . .

BECKER

I don't want to hear that, Turnbo. I got other things on my
mind.

(*to* SHEALY)

Here's Lucille's numbers. I hear Pope done hit.

SHEALY

Yeah. He hit pretty big. Say Becker, I been meaning to ask
you. I got a nephew that's trying to make something of himself. You reckon you be able to get him on down at the mill?

BECKER

I don't know if they hiring. But I'll check into it. I know some
people down there will be able to take care of him if they
hiring. I can't promise nothing but I'll talk to them for you.

SHEALY

Thanks Becker. His name is Robert Shealy. He's trying to
straighten himself out and I told his mama I'd check around
and see what I can do. Thanks again. Here go your message.

(SHEALY *hands* BECKER *a piece of page, then exits.*)

TURNBO

You don't know nothing about Shealy's nephew, I can tell
that. Boy's the biggest rogue . . . what you call a thug . . . you
ever seen. He done been down there in the work house. Him
and Jenkin's boy is the one's what broke into Taylor's bar.

BECKER

Turnbo, ain't nobody asked you nothing. You just like an
old lady, always gossiping and running off at the mouth.

TURNBO

I'm just talking what I know.
> *(The phone rings.* DOUB *enters.)*

DOUB

Say Becker, I see you got some new tires.
> (BECKER *goes to answer the phone.)*

BECKER

Yeah, I got two. Gonna get two more next week. (*into phone*) Car service. (*pause*) Wooster Street. (*pause*) Yeah I know where it's at. Black car.
> *(*YOUNGBLOOD *enters as* BECKER *exits.)*

YOUNGBLOOD

Cigar Annie standing up there in the middle of Robert Street cussing out everybody.

DOUB

Oh, yeah. Who she mad at now?

YOUNGBLOOD

She started with God and went on down the list. She cussing out the mayor, Doc Goldblum, Mr. Eli, her land-lord, the light man, gas man, telephone man, and anybody else she can think of. They got her furniture and everything sitting out on the sidewalk.

TURNBO

I knew it was gonna come to that. Everybody else done moved out of that place two months ago. The building been condemned for two years.

YOUNGBLOOD

She standing up there in the middle of the street raising up her dress.

TURNBO

I bet she ain't got no drawers on.

YOUNGBLOOD

She had traffic backed up . . . almost got hit by a milk truck . . . the cars trying to go around her but she won't let them. Standing there just throwing up her dress.

TURNBO

I don't know what she doing that for. She ain't got nothing nobody want. Now if Pearline get out there and raise up her dress . . . that be another thing. You have a riot on your hands. They ought to put Cigar Annie in Mayview. Her and Stool Pigeon both.

DOUB

Ain't nothing wrong with Cigar Annie. They had her down in Mayview two or three times. They figure anybody cuss out God and don't care who's listening got to be crazy. They found out she got more sense than they do. That's why they let her go. She raising up her dress cause that's all anybody ever wanted from her since she was twelve years old. She say if that's all you want . . . here it is.

TURNBO

She sending out an S.O.S. That's what she's doing.

DOUB

Turnbo, I don't know why I try and talk with you. Next time remind me to shut up.

YOUNGBLOOD

Say Doub, Peaches been by here?

DOUB

I ain't seen her.

YOUNGBLOOD

I'll be over at Clifford's if she comes.

DOUB

When you gonna work on my car? I thought you was gonna take a look at my car.

YOUNGBLOOD

I can't do it today. I'll take a look at it for you tomorrow.

TURNBO

If you going next door bring me back a cup of coffee.

YOUNGBLOOD

I ain't your slave. Walk over and get you own coffee.
(YOUNGBLOOD *exits.*)

TURNBO

That boy ain't got no sense.

DOUB

He all right. He's just young. Got a lot to learn. That gal keep after him, he'll be all right.

TURNBO

He don't need that gal. Don't know how to treat her. Treat her like the kind of class he is.

DOUB

You don't know what nobody need. Let that boy alone to live his life. Ain't nobody told you what you need. Always talking about somebody.

TURNBO

That ain't what I'm saying. You know that gal gonna see past that boy and go on to somebody got some sense to treat her right. Somebody that got more respect for her than to be messing around with her own sister.

DOUB

You don't know what you talking about.

TURNBO

You see he be asking about her. I seen her riding around in his car here lately. She come by here and they go off running around together. Don't even try to hide it.

DOUB

That don't mean nothing cause she was riding in his car.

TURNBO

He be calling her on the telephone too! I know what I'm talking about. You watch. That gal is gonna see right past him.

DOUB

Well let him find that out. He's got his own way to come to things. That's all I'm saying. Let the boy alone.

TURNBO

I ain't messing with him. I just say he ain't got no sense. I believe he got shell-shocked over there in Vietnam.

DOUB

Turnbo, you mess with anybody you get the chance to put your nose in their business. Let the boy live his life.

TURNBO

Remember that boy that used to be around here? What was his name . . . Jasper! That's it. Fool went crazy and jumped off the Irene Kaufman Settlement House? I told you about him when I first seen him. I told you then he ain't had no sense and I'm telling you about this boy now, and you wanna call it putting my nose in folk's business. But you mark my words. I just live and let live, but damn if I can't talk to express an opinion same as everybody else, without folks accusing me of being tied up in folk's business. I just talk what I know. Just like I told you Fielding wasn't coming back with your four dollars. He out somewhere getting drunk. I told you not to give it to him.

DOUB

See, there you go, messing in people's business.
        (The phone rings.)
I ain't give him nothing. I loaned him four dollars and you done already got you nose stuck up in it. That's my business about when he pay me.

TURNBO

I just say . . .

DOUB

Yeah, well just say it to yourself.
        *(*DOUB *exits.* TURNBO *answers the phone.)*

TURNBO

(into phone) Car service. *(pause)* Where? *(pause)* All right. Brown car. You be ready cause I ain't waiting.
        *(*TURNBO *hangs up the phone as* YOUNGBLOOD
        enters carrying a cup of coffee.)

YOUNGBLOOD

Here.

TURNBO

What's that for?

YOUNGBLOOD

That's your coffee, nigger. Give me thirty cents.

TURNBO

You told me to get my own. How you know I ain't sent somebody else?

YOUNGBLOOD

Aw, nigger, take this coffee and give me thirty cents.

TURNBO

I got a trip.

> (TURNBO *exits.* YOUNGBLOOD *sets the coffee down on the stove. The phone rings.* YOUNG-
> BLOOD *answers it.*)

YOUNGBLOOD (*into phone*)

Car service. (*pause*) Where you at? I thought you was going down to the furniture store with me. (*pause*) What's wrong with your hair? Ain't nothing wrong (*pause*) with your hair. Rudy say something was wrong with your hair? (*pause*) Naw, I ain't told her. I'm gonna wait till every-thing's settled. What time you gonna be done? (*pause*) All right, I'll pick you up at three o'clock.

> (*He hangs up the phone and dials again.*)

Mr. Harper, please. (*pause*) Darnell Williams. (*pause*) Mr. Harper? This is Darnell Williams . . . I'm calling about the house under the GI Bill . . . you said to call and get a clos-ing date. (*pause*) A title search? I thought they had the title. (*pause*) No I can understand that but I thought all of that was taken care of by the down payment? (*pause*) Well, how much? (*pause*) That's all I have to do? Ain't nothing else gonna come up? (*pause*) Two weeks! It take that long? (*pause*) No, there's no doubt I'll have it for you tomorrow. Yessir, I'll have it.

(He hangs up the phone. He takes out his notebook, looking to see how much money he has. It is obvious he does not have enough. He sits thinking when suddenly an idea occurs to him. He gets up and exits. The lights go down on the scene.)

SCENE 2

(The lights come up on the jitney station, early afternoon. BECKER *sits at his desk reading a newspaper.* TURNBO *sits downstage of him, reading a* Playboy *magazine. He holds the magazine up for* BECKER *to see.)*

TURNBO

Look at this one, Becker.
*(*BECKER *barely looks up.)*

BECKER

Yeah.

TURNBO

Boy, what a man wouldn't do with that! If I get up to heaven and she ain't there, I'm gonna ask God to send me straight to hell.
*(*YOUNGBLOOD *enters.)*

YOUNGBLOOD

Turnbo, give me my thirty cents.

TURNBO

What thirty cents you talking about?

YOUNGBLOOD

For the coffee. You know what I'm talking about.
*(*TURNBO *motions to the coffee on the stove.)*

TURNBO

There it is. I ain't touched it. That's your coffee.

YOUNGBLOOD

I know you better give me my thirty cents.

TURNBO

Boy, I ain't studying you.

YOUNGBLOOD (*in disbelief*)

You asked me to get you some coffee and now you ain't gonna pay me?

BECKER

Give the man his money, Turnbo.

TURNBO

I ain't giving him nothing.

BECKER

I ain't gonna have that dissension in here. Give the man his money!

(TURNBO *goes into his pocket.*)

TURNBO

Here. Here's your thirty cents.

(*He throws it on the floor.* YOUNGBLOOD *crosses and stands over* TURNBO, *angry.*)

YOUNGBLOOD

Pick it up!

TURNBO

It's yours. You pick it up.

YOUNGBLOOD

I ain't threw it down there.

TURNBO

Well, let it lay there then. I'm through with it.

(TURNBO *goes back to reading his magazine.* YOUNGBLOOD *backs off.*)

YOUNGBLOOD

Well, let it lay there then. But before this day is over you gonna pick up my thirty cents.

(TURNBO *suddenly jumps up and picks up the money.*)

TURNBO
Here! Here! Here's your thirty cents. You satisfied?
(*They stare at each other for a beat. The phone
rings, and* YOUNGBLOOD *moves to answer it.*
TURNBO *moves behind him.*)

TURNBO
That's my trip!

BECKER
You know that's his trip, Turnbo.

TURNBO
I thought he just come back from a trip.

YOUNGBLOOD
(*into phone*) Car service.

BECKER
He had to go downtown to take care of some business. You
know everything else I'm surprised you didn't know that.

YOUNGBLOOD
Yeah, okay. Red Chevy.
(YOUNGBLOOD *exits.*)

TURNBO
That boy ain't got good sense.

BECKER
If you leave it to you, ain't nobody got no sense.

TURNBO
They ain't! What sense it make for that McNeil boy to steal his
grandmama's television? What sense it make for Shealy's
nephew to break in Taylor's bar? What sense it make for
that boy to run with his girlfriend's sister? Half these niggers
around here running on empty and that boy at the top of the list.
(BECKER *throws the newspaper down on the
sofa and starts for the door.*)

BECKER
Turnbo, sometimes you act like a kid. If Lucille call tell
her I'm picking up the groceries. If you pass a car wash

you might want to stop in and get your car washed. What sense it make to haul people around in a dirty car?

(BECKER *exits.* TURNBO *goes back to reading his magazine. The phone rings.*)

TURNBO (*into phone*)

Car service. Youngblood? He ain't here. Who's this? Peaches? (*pause*) Yeah, I thought that was you. Naw, Youngblood ain't here. Is there anything you want me to tell him? (*pause*) Pick you up at four o'clock instead of three. Okay I'll tell him.

(*He hangs up the phone.* RENA *enters.*)

RENA

Mr. Turnbo, Darnell around here?

TURNBO

He went on a trip.

RENA

He say when he's coming back?

TURNBO

He'll be back in a minute. You may as well wait on him. How you doing? You don't come by too much no more. I remember you used to come by and see Youngblood . . . get some money to buy the baby some milk. He getting big I bet. How old is he now?

RENA

Two. Going on three. Running around, trying to talk.

TURNBO

Time just keep going. It don't wait on nobody. Everything change. I remember when you was wearing diapers. Your mother did a good job of raising you. You can tell that right off. Your mother can be proud of you. It ain't easy these days to raise a child. I don't know what's in these young boys' heads. Seem like they don't respect nobody. They don't even respect themselves. When I was coming along that was the first thing you learned. If you didn't respect yourself . . . quite naturally you couldn't respect nobody else. When I was coming along the more respect you had for other people . . . the more people respected you. Seem like it come back to you double.

These young boys don't know nothing about that . . . and it's gonna take them a lifetime to find out. They disrespect everybody and don't think nothing about it. They steal their own grandmother's television. Get hold of one woman . . . time another one walk by they grab hold to her. Don't even care who it is. It could be anybody. I just try to live and let live. My grandmother was like that. She the one raised me. She didn't care what nobody else done as long as it didn't cross her path. She was a good woman. She taught me most everything I know. She wouldn't let you lie. That was just about the worst thing you could be. A liar didn't know the truth and wasn't never gonna find out. And everybody know it's the truth what set you free. Now I ain't trying to get in your business or nothing. Like I say I just live and let live. But some things just come up on you wrong and you have to say something about it otherwise it throw your whole life off balance.

I know you don't want to hear this . . . but you don't need no hot-headed young boy like Youngblood. What you need is somebody level-headed who know how to respect and appreciate a woman . . . I can see the kind of woman you is. You ain't the kind of woman for Youngblood and he ain't the kind of man for you. You need a more mature . . . responsible man.

RENA

I don't think so.

TURNBO

You just wait awhile. You'll see that I'm right. I done seen many a young girl wake up when it's too late. Don't you be like that. You go on and find yourself a man that know how to treat you. You don't need nobody run the streets all hours of the day and night. You ain't that kind of woman.

RENA

Darnell don't run the streets. I don't know what you talking about.

TURNBO

Oh, I see him . . . running around with other women. I see him with your sister all the time. (*The phone rings.*) Day and night.

RENA

Your phone's ringing.

TURNBO

I ain't trying to get in your business now. I'm telling you
this for your own good. If you was some other kind of
woman, I wouldn't be wasting my time.

RENA

I got to go. Tell Darnell I was by to see him.
  (RENA *exits.* TURNBO *goes to answer the phone.*)

TURNBO

(*into phone*) Car service. (*pause*) Becker? Oh, hello
Lucille. He's not here right now. He said to tell you he was
going to pick up some groceries. Okay, I'll tell him.
  (*He hangs up the phone as* DOUB *enters.*)

DOUB

Fielding been back here?

TURNBO

I ain't seen him. I told you he laid up somewhere drunk on
your four dollars. You ain't gonna see him till he sober.
  (YOUNGBLOOD *enters.*)

YOUNGBLOOD

Man, these white folks is slick. (*The phone rings.*) They
think of all kind of ways to get your money.

DOUB

If you just now finding that out . . . then God help what
you don't know.
  (RENA *enters.*)

RENA

Darnell, I want to see you.

YOUNGBLOOD

What you want to see me about. I'm working, woman. I
told you about coming by my work.

DOUB

Your trip, Turnbo.

TURNBO

Naw it ain't!

DOUB

I just come back, nigger take this trip!
(TURNBO *reluctantly takes the phone.*)

TURNBO

Car service. (*pause*) Okay. Brown car. You be ready now,
cause I ain't gonna wait.
(TURNBO *hangs up and exits, followed by* DOUB.)

RENA

Darnell, I don't understand. I try so hard. I'm doing everything I can to try and make this work.

YOUNGBLOOD

What? What's the matter?

RENA

I'm working my little job down there at the restaurant . . .
going to school . . . trying to take care of Jesse . . . trying
to take care of your needs . . . trying to keep the house
together . . . trying to make everything better. Now, I come
home from work I got to go to the store. I go upstairs and
look in the drawer and the food money is gone. Now you
explain that to me. There was eighty dollars in the drawer
that ain't in there now.

YOUNGBLOOD

I needed it. I'm gonna put it back.

RENA

What you need it for? You tell me. What's more important
than me and Jesse eating?

YOUNGBLOOD

I had to pay a debt. I'm gonna put it back.

RENA

You know I don't touch the grocery money. Whatever hap-
pens we got to eat. If I need clothes . . . I do without. My little
personal stuff . . . I do without. If I ain't got no electricity . . .
I do without . . . but I don't never touch the grocery money.
Cause I'm not gonna be that irresponsible to my child. Cause
he depend on me. I'm not going to be that irresponsible to
my family. I ain't gonna be like that. Jesse gonna have a

chance at life. He ain't going to school hungry cause I spent the grocery money on some nail polish or some Afro Sheen. He ain't gonna be laying up in the bed hungry and unable to sleep cause his daddy took the grocery money to pay a debt.

YOUNGBLOOD

Aw, woman I try and do what's right and this is what I get.

RENA

You know what you be doing better than I but whatever it is it ain't enough.

YOUNGBLOOD

What you talking about now? I told you I'm gonna put the money back.

RENA

It ain't all about the money, Darnell. I'm talking about the way you been doing. You ain't never home no more.

YOUNGBLOOD

I be working. You know I'm out here hustling. I got two jobs looking for three.

RENA

You be out half the night. I wake up and you ain't there.

YOUNGBLOOD

That's what time the people say come to work! Two A.M. to six A.M. I can't tell UPS what to do! What time to have people come to work. I told you that when I took the job. I told you that I wouldn't be home. You said okay. Now you wanna come with this about me not being home. You know where I'm at.

RENA

You say you working at UPS but I don't never see no UPS money.

YOUNGBLOOD

I had some debts to pay. I told you that too. I told you I wouldn't see no money for awhile.

RENA

What kind of debt?

YOUNGBLOOD

Look baby, just hang with me awhile. That's all I ask. Just
for a minute.

RENA

I been hanging with you! That's what you said last time.
"Hang with me and it'll all turn around." When's it gonna
turn around, Darnell?

YOUNGBLOOD

Soon, baby. Soon. Just hang with me.

RENA

I just want you to know I ain't no fool, Darnell. I know you
been running around with Peaches and her crowd all hours of
the night. Doing whatever you be doing. I may not know
everything but I know something's going on. I know you all
doing something.

YOUNGBLOOD

Who told you that? Me and Peaches doing what?

RENA

She's my sister, Darnell. Don't you think I can tell she's
trying to hide something from me.

YOUNGBLOOD

Hide what? What you talking about? Hide what? What she
trying to hide?

RENA

Ain't no need in you bothering to come home cause I just
might not be there when you get there.
> (RENA *exits. The phone rings.* YOUNGBLOOD
> *starts to go after her, changes his mind and
> comes back and stands in the middle of the
> room perplexed. Suddenly he takes his note-
> book from his pocket and throws it on the floor.
> He regains his composure, picks up the book
> and exits.* BECKER *enters on the fourth ring.*)

BECKER (*into phone*)

Car service. (*pause*) Shealy don't work here!
> (BECKER *slams the phone down as* DOUB *enters.*)

DOUB

I was just talking to Clifford next door. He say the man is gonna board his place up next month.

BECKER

Yeah, I know. The man from the city was by here two weeks ago, too. They're gonna tear it all down, this whole block.

DOUB

The man was by here and you ain't told nobody! What he say?

BECKER

They're gonna board the place up first of next month.

DOUB

Why in the hell didn't you tell somebody!

BECKER

I'm telling you now.

DOUB

Fine time to tell me, two weeks later. It ain't like that's a small piece of news. I got rent to pay. Doctor bills. Every man in here depending on this station for their livelihood. The city's gonna board it up . . . you've known for two weeks . . . and you ain't bothered to get around to telling nobody. That ain't like you Becker. What we gonna do now? In the two weeks we got.

BECKER

I don't know. I kinda figured we'd all just go in together somewhere else. Find another place. But I don't know now. I'm just tired, Doub. Can't hardly explain it none. You look up one day and all you got left is what you ain't spent. Everyday cost you something and you don't all the time realize it.

I used to question God about everything. Why he hardened Pharaoh's heart? Why he let Jacob steal his brother's birthright? After Coreen died I told myself I wasn't gonna ask no more questions. Cause the answers didn't matter. They didn't matter right then. I thought that would change but it never did. It still don't matter after all these years. It don't look like it's never gonna matter. I'm tired of waiting for God to decide whether he want to hold my hand. I been running cars out of here for eighteen years and I think I'm just tired of driving.

DOUB

I been with you for twelve of them eighteen years and I
would have thought you would have told me we was
gonna have to move cause they boarding up the station.

BECKER

I'm telling you now.

DOUB

That ain't what I mean, Becker. It's like you just a shadow
of yourself. The station done gone downhill. Some people
overcharge. Some people don't haul. Fielding stay drunk.
I just watch you and you don't do nothing.

BECKER

What's to be done? I try to keep cars running out of here and
keep everybody happy. I post the rates up on the board. If
somebody charge extra and people complain, I give them the
difference and tell the driver about it. I ain't gonna put
nobody out unless they totally irresponsible. As for Fielding,
I don't let him drink in here, but I can't tell the man about his
personal business unless people start to complain.

DOUB

Complain? Hell, they don't do no complaining. They just call
somebody else. Somebody ask them for a number, they don't
give them Court 1-9802. They give them somebody else's
number. Complain? You think they're gonna call you up and
complain? Nigger, they don't even know you're alive.

BECKER

I just do the best I can do.

DOUB

Sometime your best ain't enough.
          (TURNBO *enters.*)

DOUB

Turnbo, they boarding up the station the first of the month.
Becker talking about quitting, so we ought to start thinking
about moving somewhere or getting on with somebody else.

TURNBO

Who's boarding up the station?

DOUB

The city. They fixing to tear down the whole block. Clifford and everybody done got their notices. The man was by here two weeks ago.

TURNBO

So that's what they was doing! I seen them snooping around here. Told me they was conducting a survey. Well, what we gonna do? Becker, you quitting?

BECKER

I ain't said I was quitting.

DOUB

That's what you told me.

BECKER

I said I was thinking about it.
    (*The phone rings.*)

DOUB

We ought to have a meeting and figure out one way or another what we gonna do.

TURNBO

They never could leave well enough alone.
    (TURNBO *answers the phone.*)
Car service. (*pause*) Oh hello Lucille, he's here. Just a minute. Becker!
    (*He hands* BECKER *the phone.*)
They won't be satisfied until they tear the whole goddamn neighborhood down!

BECKER

(*into phone*) Becker here. (*pause*) Yeah, I know, Lucille. (*pause*) Tomorrow? I thought it wasn't until next month. Who called? (*pause*) Are you sure? (*pause*) Yeah, well okay. I'll talk to you.
    (BECKER *hangs up the phone.*)

TURNBO

They gonna board up the place tomorrow!

BECKER

My boy's getting out tomorrow.

(*The lights go down on the scene.*)

SCENE 3

(The lights come up on the jitney station, early the following morning. It is obvious YOUNGBLOOD *has spent the night there. He sits on the couch figuring in his notebook.)*

*(*TURNBO *enters.)*

TURNBO

You seen Becker this morning?

YOUNGBLOOD

He ain't come in yet.

TURNBO

You know his boy's getting out today?

YOUNGBLOOD

Yeah. Getting out of where?

TURNBO

You don't know about Becker's son?

YOUNGBLOOD

Know what?

TURNBO

Becker's boy been in the penitentiary for twenty years. He's getting out today.

YOUNGBLOOD

I ain't even knew Becker had a son.

TURNBO

Been in the penitentiary for twenty years! Right down
there at the Western State Pen, and Becker ain't never been
down there to see him once!

YOUNGBLOOD

Yeah?

TURNBO

I think it's a shame, Becker just wrote him off his list.

YOUNGBLOOD

Yeah. Well, that's his business, I guess.

TURNBO

Hell! That's his own son and if he ain't gonna stand by
him, who's gonna? He ain't got nobody else. It killed his
mama. Lucille ain't none of his mama. His mama died
about a month after he went in. When the judge sentenced
him to the electric chair, his mama just fell dead away.
They brought her home and put her in the bed, and she laid
right up there till she died.

YOUNGBLOOD

Gave him the electric chair?

TURNBO

That's right. Sure did. I was there! He later got it com-
muted to life.

YOUNGBLOOD

What he do to get the electric chair?

TURNBO

See, Becker's boy . . . Clarence is his name but everybody call
him Booster . . . See now, Booster he liked that science. You know
the science fair that they have over at the Buhel Planetarium every
year where they have all them science experiments where they
make the water run uphill and things like that? Booster won first
place three years in a row. He the only one who ever did that. I
can't even count how many times he had his picture in the paper.
They let him in to the University of Pittsburgh. You know back
then they didn't have too many colored out there, but they was trying to catch up to the Russians and they didn't care if he was col-

ored or not. Gave him a scholarship and everything. Becker was just as proud as he could be. Him and Booster was always close. Becker used to take him hunting down around Wheeling West Virginia. They go hunting and fishing. Becker didn't have but the one boy. After he was born the doctor told his wife that if she had another one it was liable to kill her. Say she was lucky to have the one. Anyway, Booster goes out to Pitt there and he meets this old white gal. Young gal . . . about eighteen she was. Of course Booster wasn't about nineteen himself. Now her old man was some kind of big shot down there at Gulf Oil. Had a lot of money and had done bought the gal a car for her birthday. Booster and that gal . . . they just go everywhere together. She ride him around like she was his chauffeur. Of course, she let him drive it too. I believe he drove it more than she did. That gal was crazy about Booster, and they was just sneaking around and sneaking around, you know. She didn't want her daddy to know she was fooling around with no colored boy. Well, one day see her father was up here in the neighborhood looking for one of them whores. He find one and she tell him to drive up the dead-end street there by the school, so she can turn the trick in the car. Don't you know they pulled right up in back of this gal's car where her and Booster done went to fool around! Her father recognizes the car and he goes over and looks inside and there's Booster just banging the hell out of his daughter! Well, that cracker went crazy.

He just couldn't stand the sight of Booster screwing that gal and went to yanking open the car door. Booster didn't know who he was. All he knew was some crazy white man done opened the door and was screaming his head off. He proceeded to beat the man half to death. To get to the short of it . . . the police come and the gal said that she was driving downtown on her way home from a movie, and when she stopped for a red light, Booster jumped into her car and made her drive up there on the dead-end street . . . where he raped her. They arrested Booster and Becker got him out on bail cause he knew the gal was lying. The first day he was out . . . the first day! . . . he went over to that gal's house and shot her dead right on the front porch.

YOUNGBLOOD

Served the bitch right!

TURNBO

What you talking about! I knew you ain't had no sense. I don't know why I try and talk to you.

YOUNGBLOOD
Served her right for lying!
(The phone rings.)

TURNBO
That ain't no cause to kill nobody! I don't care if she was lying. See, that's what's wrong with you young folks. Don't take time to stop and think before you speak. "Serve the bitch right!" That's all you know.

YOUNGBLOOD
It does!

TURNBO
Fool! What is you talking about? That boy ain't had no right to kill that gal!

YOUNGBLOOD
She lied on him, didn't she?

TURNBO
That gal you got have a right to kill you cause you lyin' to her?

YOUNGBLOOD
We ain't talking about me. Stay out of my business!

TURNBO
Your business is already in the street. Everybody know how you misuse that gal, keeping her tied up in the house with that baby while you run around with her sister and don't give her two pennies to buy the baby no milk.
(YOUNGBLOOD, enraged, rushes TURNBO and grabs him in the collar.)

YOUNGBLOOD
You stay the fuck out of my business!

TURNBO
Now you wanna beat me up for telling the truth. Well, go ahead, I'm an old man. Go ahead, it'll make you proud to hit an old man.
(YOUNGBLOOD tries to restrain himself.)

YOUNGBLOOD
You stay out my business, Turnbo. I'm warning you!

TURNBO

I done told you your business is in the street.

*(*YOUNGBLOOD *loses control and punches* TURN-BO *in the mouth. The blow knocks* TURNBO *to the floor and bloodies his mouth.* TURNBO *gets up and glares at* YOUNGBLOOD. TURNBO *starts out the door just as* BECKER *enters.)*

YOUNGBLOOD

You just stay the fuck out of my business!

BECKER

What's going on?

*(*BECKER *notices* TURNBO*'s bloody mouth.)*

BECKER

What happened, Turnbo?

YOUNGBLOOD

You tell him to stay out of my business and everything will be straight. I don't get in his business and I don't want him in mine.

TURNBO

You know what I done already told you.

*(*YOUNGBLOOD *tries to get to* TURNBO, *but* BECK-ER *is in between the two of them.)*

BECKER

Hold it! Hold it! What's going on here?

*(*YOUNGBLOOD *strains to get at* TURNBO.*)*

YOUNGBLOOD

This motherfucker . . . got his nose . . . all up in my business.

TURNBO

Let him go, Becker. I ain't scared of him. All I did was tell him where his business was. In the gutter!

*(*YOUNGBLOOD *starts toward* TURNBO. BECKER *grabs him.* YOUNGBLOOD *struggles to get free.)*

YOUNGBLOOD

Let me go. Becker! Let me go!

BECKER

Hold it, Youngblood! There ain't gonna be no more fight-

ing in here! Go on, Turnbo. I'll take care of him. You go on.
(TURNBO *exits.*)

BECKER

What done got in you, boy. Hitting an old man like that. I
can't have you fighting and causing trouble. You and
Turnbo don't get along . . . just don't speak to him.

YOUNGBLOOD

I don't want him talking and speaking rumors about my
business. That's all! That's all I want!
(TURNBO *kicks open the door and throws a pistol on* YOUNGBLOOD. *He is very excited.*)

TURNBO

You don't believe your business is in the street! Is that
right! Is that right!

BECKER

Turnbo!

TURNBO

Come on! You young punk! Come on! Hit me again! You
don't believe that your business is in the street. I'll tell you
something else. I done had that gal of yours.

YOUNGBLOOD

You lying motherfucker!

BECKER

Put that gun up, Turnbo!

TURNBO

Yeah. Come on! Jump at me! And I'll blow your ass to
kingdom come!
(YOUNGBLOOD *stops.*)

YOUNGBLOOD

You lying motherfucker!

TURNBO

You think I'm lying, huh! I'll tell you how much I'm
lying.
(BECKER *moves in between them.*)

BECKER

Yeah, you lying. Why you wanna tell that boy that lie? That gal ain't give you the time of day.

TURNBO

Stay out of this, Becker!

BECKER

Don't lie to the boy like that.
(He moves toward TURNBO.*)*
Come on now, put the gun up.

YOUNGBLOOD

Just because you used to them lowlife women don't mean everybody else is.
*(*TURNBO *cocks back the hammer.)*

TURNBO

You keep it up! You keep it up!

BECKER

You don't want to do that now; it ain't worth all that. Come on, Turnbo. The boy ain't meant nothing. He just young and foolish. I'll straighten him up. He just young. He don't know no better. Come on, put that gun up.

TURNBO

Boy, you got one more time to mess with me again! Just one more time!
*(*TURNBO *puts the gun back in his pocket.* BECKER *guides* TURNBO *to the door, and they exit together.* YOUNGBLOOD *stands motionless in the middle of the room.* BECKER *enters.)*

BECKER

Goddamn! If it ain't one thing it's another. Youngblood, you stay away from Turnbo! Just stay out of his way!

YOUNGBLOOD

I ain't studying him. That gun don't scare me.

BECKER

I ain't asked you was you studying him.

YOUNGBLOOD
When they made one gun they didn't stop making them.

BECKER
Just stay clear of him and don't say nothing to him. You can't go around hitting everybody that don't see eye to eye with you. Turnbo carry that gun in his car and if you push him far enough he'll run out there and get it. That ain't the first time. One of these days he's gonna use it. (*The phone rings.*) So you just stay clear of him. The less words you have with Turnbo the better.
   (BECKER *answers the phone.*)
(*into phone*) Car service. (*pause*) Where you going? (*pause*) All right. Red Chevy.
   (FIELDING *enters.*)

FIELDING
Hey, Youngblood. Becker, what happened to Turnbo? He's sitting out there in his car cussing up a blue streak.

BECKER (*to* YOUNGBLOOD)
Eighteen forty-five Bedford. They're going to the bus station.

YOUNGBLOOD
I ain't carrying no suitcases in my car, Becker.

BECKER
You are if you want to jitney out of here.
   (FIELDING *gets the drift of what is happening.*)

FIELDING
What's the address? I'll make the trip.

BECKER
It's Youngblood's trip and he's gonna pull his weight around here.

YOUNGBLOOD
What you mean pull my weight? I pull my weight. I just don't want to mess up my car.

BECKER
How in the hell is putting somebody's suitcase in your trunk gonna mess up your car? That's what it's designed for! I done it for eighteen years and ain't never messed up my car. You talk like a fool.

FIELDING

Let me go, Becker.

YOUNGBLOOD

What's the address?

BECKER

Eighteen forty-five Bedford.
(YOUNGBLOOD *exits.*)

FIELDING

Why you wanna force that boy to haul things when he
don't want to?

BECKER

Stay out of this, Fielding. It ain't none of your business.

FIELDING

I just asked cause I don't see much sense in it. If the boy
don't want to haul people's things, he's got a right not to
haul them, the way I see it. I ain't getting into nothing.
(TURNBO *enters.*)

TURNBO

Becker! You better straighten up that young fool before I
be done killed him! I told you all along that boy ain't got
no sense! Punching me in my mouth!

BECKER

I done talked to him, Turnbo.

FIELDING

Youngblood hit you? You all been fighting? What was you
all fighting about?

TURNBO

He's got one more time! I'm telling you, Becker! Damn
fool gonna hit me cause I tell him the truth. He is fooling
around with that gal's sister and everybody knows it!

FIELDING

Who, Peaches?

TURNBO

I done seen him and her sister riding around here more

than one time. He leave that gal at home to take care of the
baby while he run around in the street with her sister. How
many times you seen her come by here to try and track him
down so she can get some money to buy that baby some
milk? How many times you seen her?

(FIELDING *opens a bottle and begins to drink.*)

FIELDING

Oh, I seen her by here before.

BECKER

Turnbo, you might come out better if you stayed out of
people's business.

TURNBO

I ain't in nobody's business. We was having a conversation and
it come up. I just speak my mind. I ain't never been one to bite
my tongue about expressing an opinion and I ain't gonna start
now. The only thing is, you better get that boy straightened out.

(BECKER *notices* FIELDING *drinking.*)

BECKER

Fielding! Goddamn it! I done told you about drinking in here!

FIELDING

I was just having a little nip, Becker.

BECKER

Well, that's it! I can't have you drinking and running jitneys out of here! That's it, your time is up! You done run
you last jitney out of here!

FIELDING

What you talking about?

BECKER

You heard me. I know I speak clearly enough.

FIELDING

(*apologizing*) I ain't done nothing. I just had a little nip.

BECKER

I told you time and again about drinking in the station.
That's it! I ain't got no more conversation for you.

FIELDING

You see this, Turnbo?

BECKER (*to* TURNBO)

Fielding is out! I don't want him running no more trips out of here. I told him time and again about that drinking.

FIELDING

What is you talking about? (*The phone rings.*) I paid my monthly dues and the month ain't up yet. I ain't going nowhere!
(BECKER *takes some money out of his pocket.*)

BECKER

Here. Here's your money.
(FIELDING *doesn't take the money. and* BECKER *lays it down on top of the stove.*)

BECKER

There's your money. Take it and get out of here.

FIELDING

I ain't taking nothing. I paid for two more weeks, and two more weeks is what I get.

BECKER

There's your money. Now we straight.
(BECKER *answers the phone.*)
(*into phone*) Car service. (*pause*) Twenty-seven nineteen Francis Street Projects? Be right there. Turnbo, take that trip.
(TURNBO *starts to exit.*)

FIELDING

That's my trip, Turnbo!

BECKER

I done told you, you ain't running no more trips out of this station. Take your money and get out.

FIELDING

Who the hell do you think you are? You ain't running over me, Becker!

BECKER

Take your money and get out. Go on, Turnbo.

TURNBO

I don't want to get in the middle of this. I don't want to be in nobody's business.

BECKER

I'll take it. (*to* FIELDING) You just be gone when I get back.
        (BECKER *exits.* FIELDING *calls after him.*)

FIELDING

This is a free country! I'm a free man! You can't tell me what to do! This is the United States of America.
        (*He takes another drink.*)
You see that, Turnbo? You see that?

(*The lights fade to black.*)

SCENE 4

(The lights come up on the jitney station a half-hour later. TURNBO *and* FIELDING *have been joined by* BOOSTER, *who stands looking out the window. He is dressed in his prison-issued suit, and wears a white shirt without a tie.)*

FIELDING

Yeah, I know your daddy real good. I've been driving jit-neys with him for eight years now. And I worked off and on with him when he was down at the mill too. That's when I was younger. Here, get yourself a nip.
(He drinks from the bottle and offers it to BOOSTER, *who declines.)*

BOOSTER

No thanks. You say he should be back in a minute?

TURNBO

He just went out on a short trip. He'll be back in no time. Things done changed since the last time you seen them, I reckon.

BOOSTER

Yeah, pretty much.

TURNBO

They're tearing everything down around here. All along Wylie there. You see they done tore everything down. They gonna tear this building down. They gonna board it up first of the month. We're gonna have to move. Either that or split up. We can't stay here no more.

FIELDING

You got to have somebody you can count on you know. Now my wife . . . we been separated for twenty-two years now . . . but I ain't never loved nobody the way I loved that woman. You know what I mean?

BOOSTER

Yeah, I know.

FIELDING

She the only thing in the world that I got. I had a dream once. It just touched me so. I was climbing this ladder. It was a solid gold ladder and I was climbing up into heaven. I get to the top of the ladder and I can see all the saints sitting around . . . and I could see her too . . . sitting there in her place in glory. Just as I reached the top my hand started to slip and I called out for help. All them saints and angels . . . St. Peter and everybody . . . they just sat there and looked at me. She was the only one who left her seat in glory and tried to help me to keep from falling back down that ladder. I ain't never forgot that. When I woke up . . . tears was all over my face, just running all down in my ears and I laid there and cried like a baby . . . cause that meant so much to me. To find out after all these years, that she still loved me.

BOOSTER

That's some heavy drama, my man.

FIELDING

Oh, she love me all right. I know she do. I ain't seen that woman in twenty-two years . . . but I know she loves me.
(FIELDING *takes another drink as* BECKER *enters and stands in the doorway glaring at* FIELDING.)

FIELDING

Hey Becker. I was just talking to your son.

BECKER

I thought I told you not to be here when I got back.
(FIELDING *staggers to his feet.*)

FIELDING

All right, Becker. You win. I'm gone.
(FIELDING *starts toward the door.* BECKER *crosses to the stove and picks up the money.*)

BECKER

Here. Take your money with you.
(FIELDING *takes the money and starts to exit. He
stops.*)

FIELDING

Let me work the two weeks. I'll be sober in the morning.
It's almost over, Becker. It's almost over.

BECKER

Go on home, Fielding. I'll see you tomorrow. You be sober
when you come in here.
(FIELDING *starts to exit.* BECKER *holds out his
hand for the money.* FIELDING *gives it to him
and exits.* BECKER *turns to face* BOOSTER.)

BOOSTER

How you doing, Pop?
(BOOSTER *holds out his hand.* BECKER *takes it
awkwardly.*)

BECKER

Fine. Fine. How you doing? You look good.

BOOSTER

I feel pretty good. Lucille told me you'd be down here.

BECKER

Turnbo, go next door and tell Clifford to send me one of
them fish sandwiches, will you?
(TURNBO *exits reluctantly.*)

BECKER

So you doing all right huh?

BOOSTER

I don't know. I been looking around. I don't know what to
think. People going everywhere. All up and down. Dogs
and cats. Airplanes. It's gonna take me a while to get used
to things.

BECKER

So what you gonna do with the rest of your life now that
you done ruined it?

BOOSTER

Hey, Pop . . . I just stopped by to say hi. See how you doing.

BECKER

Can't get no job. Who's gonna hire you? You got a mark on you a foot wide. They can see you coming. You just took your life and threw it away like it wasn't worth nothing.

BOOSTER

I don't want all this. I don't want to hear about my life being ruined. I just stopped by to say hi. I don't want this. I done paid my debt.

BECKER

You don't even know where your debt begins.

BOOSTER

I know where it ended. It ended after I did them twenty years. I don't owe nobody nothing. They tried to give me that parole five years ago and I turned it down because I didn't want to owe nobody nothing. I didn't want nobody looking after me telling me what to do . . . asking me questions about my life. I walk in here to say hi and you start telling me my life is ruined. How I'm gonna get a job . . . I don't want that, Pop. I'm a grown man. I'm thirty-nine years old. I'm young. I'm healthy. I ain't got no complaints . . . and I don't carry no grudges. Whatever was between us these twenty years I put aside. I don't hold no grudge.

BECKER

Who the hell care what you hold? I'm the one got to walk around here with people pointing at me. Talking about me behind my back. "There go his father. That's him." People trying to sneak a look at me out the corner of their eye. See if they can see something wrong with me. If they can see what kind of man would raise a boy to do something like that. You done marked me and you walk in here talking about you ain't got no grudge!

BOOSTER

I'm just saying I don't have no hard feeling that you didn't come to see me, Pop. I been thinking about my life and all the things you did for me . . . all the things you gave me . . . all the things you taught me. All the things . . .

BECKER

Everything I give you . . . you threw away. You ain't got nothing now. You got less than the day you was born. Then you had some dignity. Some innocence . . . You ain't got nothing now. You took and you threw it all away. You thirty-nine years old and you ain't got nothing.

BOOSTER

Naw Pop, you wrong. I may have lost some things. I may have missed some things . . . but that don't mean I ain't got nothing.

BECKER

You ain't got nothing boy!

BOOSTER

Well, since we talking about what we got . . . what you got, Pop? You the boss of a jitney station.

BECKER

I am the boss of a jitney station. I'm a deacon down at the church. Got me a little house. It ain't much but it's mine. I worked twenty-seven years at the mill . . . got me a pension. I got a wife. I got respect. I can walk anywhere and hold my head up high. What I ain't got is a son that did me honor . . . The Bible say "Honor thy father and thy mother." I ain't got that. I ain't got a son I can be proud of. That's what I ain't got. A son to come up behind me . . . living a good honest decent life. I got a son who people point to and say, "That's Becker's boy. That's the one that killed that gal. That's Becker's boy. The one they gave the electric chair. That's Becker's boy."

BOOSTER

I did what I had to do and I paid for it.

BECKER

What you had to do! What you had to do! What law is there say you have to kill somebody if they tell a lie on you? Where does it say that? If somebody tell a lie on you, you have to kill them? Who taught you that? It was a lie! The gal told a lie! If it was the truth then go ahead and kill yourself. Go on and throw your life away. But it was a lie! We could have fought the lie. I'd already lined up a lawyer . . . together we could have fought the lie.

BOOSTER

A lawyer wasn't gonna make no difference. I wasn't going
to the penitentiary for nothing. I wasn't gonna live a lie.

BECKER

I taught you two wrongs don't make a right.

BOOSTER

Sometime they do. Sometime you got to add it up that way.
Otherwise it's just one wrong after another and you never
get to what's right. I wasn't gonna hang no sign around my
neck say rapist.

BECKER

You gonna hang one say murderer? That's better?

BOOSTER

That's honest.

BECKER

That gal lying didn't make you wrong in the world. A lie
don't make you wrong in the world.

BOOSTER

It don't make you right either. Right is right and right don't
wrong nobody. You taught me that.

BECKER

I taught you to respect life. I taught you all of life is precious.

BOOSTER

Yeah Pop, you taught me a lot of things. And a lot of things
I had to learn on my own. Like that time Mr. Rand came to
the house to collect the rent when we was two months
behind. I don't remember what year it was. I just know it
was winter. Grandma Ada had just died and you got behind
in the rent cause you had to help pay for her funeral.
    I don't know if you knew it Pop, but you were a big man.
Everywhere you went people treated you like a big man.
You used to take me to the barbershop with you. You'd
walk in there and fill up the whole place. Everybody would
stop cussing because Jim Becker had walked in. I would
just look at you and wonder how you could be that big. I
wanted to be like that. I would go to school and try to make
myself feel big. But I never could. I told myself that's okay

. . . when I get grown I'm gonna be big like that. Walk into the barbershop and have everybody stop and look at me.

That day when Mr. Rand came to the house it was snowing. You came out on the porch and he started shouting and cussing and threatening to put us out in the street where we belonged.

I was waiting for you to tell him to shut up . . . to get off your porch. But you just looked at him and promised you would have the money next month. Mama came to the door and Mr. Rand kept shouting and cussing. I looked at mama . . . she was trying to get me to go in the house . . . and I looked at you . . . and you had got smaller. The longer he shouted the smaller you got. When we went back to the barbershop you didn't seem so big no more. You was the same size as everybody else. You was just another man in the barbershop. That's when I told myself if I ever got big I wouldn't let nothing make me small.

Then when I met Susan McKnight and found out her daddy was the vice-president of Gulf Oil . . . that's when I got big. That made me a big man. I felt like I was somebody. I felt like I could walk in the barbershop and fill it up the way you did. Then when she told that lie on me that's when I woke up. That's when I realized that I wasn't big from the inside. I wasn't big on my own. When she told that lie it made me small. I wanted to do something that said I wasn't just another nigger . . . that I was Clarence Becker. I wanted to make them remember my name. And I thought about you standing there and getting small and Mr. Rand shouting and Susan McKnight shouting out that lie and I realized it was my chance to make the Beckers big again . . . my chance to show what I had learned on my own. I thought you would understand. I thought you would be proud of me.

BECKER

Proud of you for killing somebody!

BOOSTER

No, Pop. For being a warrior. For dealing with the world in ways that you didn't or couldn't or wouldn't.

BECKER

Boy, you trying to say I had something to do with you pulling that trigger. You trying to say that it's all my fault because I didn't knock Mr. Rand on his ass so I could keep a roof over your head. So you wouldn't have to sleep in the street, in the cold and the snow.

BOOSTER

No Pop, I did it.

BECKER

You gonna knock Mr. Rand on his ass for me by killing that gal.

BOOSTER

No Pop, it was for me. I did it for myself. But it didn't add up the way I thought it would. I was wrong. I can see that now.

BECKER

You could have been something. You had every advantage . . . I tried to fix it so you didn't have to follow up behind me . . . So you could go on and go further. So you could have a better life. I did without so you could have.

BOOSTER

Hey Pop, you took your road . . . you made your choices, you done what was right for you. I made my choice. I took my road and I did what was right for me. I paid the consequences. Now that's over and done. Let's just say I stopped by to say hi and leave it at that.

(BOOSTER *starts to exit.*)

BECKER

You want to know why I never came to see you?

BOOSTER

No, I don't want to know. That's your business.

BECKER

I kept seeing your face at your mother's funeral. How you just stood there and never shed a tear. Stood there with a scowl on your face. And now you want to come in here and ridicule me cause I didn't knock Mr. Rand on his ass. You wanna know why? I'll tell you why. Because I had your black ass crying to be fed. Crying to have a roof over your head. To have clothes to wear to school and lunch money in your pocket. That's why! Because I had a family. I had responsibility. If I had knocked him on his ass you would have went hungry. You wouldn't have had clothes on your back or a roof over your head. I done what I had to do. I swallowed my pride and let them mess over me, all the time saying, "You bastards got it

coming. Look out! Becker's boy's coming to straighten this
shit out! You're not gonna fuck over him! He's gonna grow
big and strong! Watch out for Becker's boy! Becker's taking
this ass whipping so his boy can stride through this shit like
Daniel in the lion's den! Watch out for Becker's boy!"
    (BECKER *has worked himself into a frenzy and is
    now near tears.*)
And what I get, huh? You tell me. What I get? Tell me
what I get! Tell me! What I get? What I get, huh?
    (BOOSTER *moves toward him.*)

BOOSTER

Pop . . .

BECKER

Stay away from me! What I get, huh? What I get? Tell me?
    (BOOSTER *is silent.*)
I get a murderer, that's what. A murderer.

BOOSTER

Pop, look . . .

BECKER

And the way your mama loved you. You killed her! You
know that? You a double murderer!

BOOSTER

I ain't killed her, Pop. You know that.

BECKER

What you call it? That woman took sick the day that judge
sentenced you and she ain't never walked or said another
word or ate another thing for twenty-three days. She just
laid up in that room until she died. Now you tell me that
ain't killing her. Tell me that ain't killing her!

BOOSTER

Every day Mama came to that courtroom by herself. Where
was you? Anybody could see how it was wearing her down.
Where was you when she needed somebody to hold her
hand . . . when she needed a shoulder to cry on . . . somebody to talk to? Where was you . . . not for me . . . but for
her . . . the woman you loved? When she fainted in that
courtroom I tried to get to her . . . but I had six deputies
holding me back. What was holding you? Where was you

them twenty-three days when she was dying?

BECKER

I was trying to keep her alive. Trying to get her to eat
something . . . trying to get her . . .

BOOSTER

It wasn't about eating, Pop. That's not what she needed . . .
a bowl of soup. She needed to know that you were there for
her. That you would be there for her when she got up. That
she could count on you to support her. But you turned your
back. Clinging to your rules . . .

BECKER

Don't you say nothing to me about turning my back!

BOOSTER

What you call it?

BECKER

I was there! I was holding her hand when she died. Where
were you? Locked up in a cage like some animal. That's what
killed her. To hear the judge say that the life she brought in
the world was unfit to live. That you be "remanded to the cus-
tody of the Commissioner of Corrections at Western State
Penitentiary and there to be executed in the electric chair.
This order to be carried out thirty days from today." Ain't that
what the judge said? Ain't that what she heard? "This order
to be carried out thirty days from today." That's what killed
her. She didn't want to live them thirty days. She didn't want
to be alive to hear on the eleven o'clock news that they had
killed you. So don't you say nothing to me about turning my
back when I nursed that woman, talked to her, held her hand,
prayed over her and the last words to come out of her mouth
was your name. I was there! Where were you Mr. Murderer?
Mr. Unfit to Live Amongst Society. Where were you when
your mama was dying and calling your name?
    (BECKER *stops and takes a moment to gather
    himself.*)
    You are my son. I helped to bring you into this world. But
from this moment on . . . I'm calling the deal off. You ain't
nothing to me, boy. You just another nigger on the street.

(BECKER *exits.* BOOSTER *stands looking down at the floor. The phone
rings. The lights go down to black.*)

ACT TWO

SCENE 1

(The lights come up on the jitney station. It is the next day. DOUB *sits in one of the chairs reading a newspaper.* TURNBO *looks at a magazine.)*

TURNBO
Now here's another something I don't understand. Lena Horne. How come everybody say she pretty? I even hear some people say she's the prettiest woman in the world.

DOUB
I ain't gonna say all that. But if she ain't, she right up there.

TURNBO
She ain't as pretty as Sarah Vaughn.

DOUB
Naw. Naw. We talking about Lena Horne. Some things just ain't open to debate. Lena Horne being pretty is one of them.

TURNBO
Sarah Vaughn got more nature than Lena Horne.

DOUB
What's that supposed to mean? Even if she do . . . how you gonna measure it? It ain't like saying she got more hair or something.

TURNBO

She got a prettier smile too. A lot of people sleeping on
Sarah Vaughn.

DOUB

How you know how many people sleeping with her?

TURNBO

I said sleeping on her, not with her. Everybody talking
about Lena Horne and people sleeping on Sarah Vaughn.
People don't know Sarah Vaughn got more of everything
than Lena Horne. They just believe what they hear. But
Sarah Vaughn got more nature . . . got a prettier smile . . .
got more personality . . . and she can sing better.

DOUB

We ain't said nothing about that. We ain't said nothing
about singing. You said Lena Horne wasn't pretty.

TURNBO

She ain't. She ain't as pretty as people think. People just
think she's pretty.

DOUB

Oh, I see . . . people just think dogs bite. People just think
if you cut yourself you'll bleed.
    (FIELDING *enters.*)
Hey Fielding . . . Turnbo say Lena Horne ain't pretty.

FIELDING

Some people say shit don't stink. Sooner or later they
gonna find out otherwise. It's them pretty women like
Lena Horne get a man killed.

TURNBO

You ain't got to be pretty to get a man killed. Any woman
will get a man killed if he ain't careful. Am I right, Doub?

DOUB

You right. That's why I don't talk about women. I don't
talk about money either. Them is the two things you never
hear me talk about too much. Them is the two things that
get most people killed.

FIELDING

Women and money will get a preacher killed.

DOUB

I seen it happen. You go and ask one of them fellows, say "Why you do that?" You have to catch him after he cooled down. You have to get him down there in jail after about six or nine months and you ask him why he killed so and so. And he'll tell you. He'll tell you he had a woman stay on his mind and he couldn't think right. Then when he seen somebody else talking to her seem like they was the cause of all his trouble . . . wasn't nothing left to do but kill him. That's why if you see me talking to a woman you can bet it's my sister or my aunt.

TURNBO

You right. The first thing a man do when he get a woman he don't want nobody else to have her. He say this is mine. I'm gonna hold on to this. I'm gonna go over and see Betty Jean but I'm gonna hold on to this. If I catch anybody sneaking around her sniffing . . . I'm gonna bust his nose and break both of his legs . . . if I don't shoot him with my forty-four. He say that and then he go on over to Betty Jean. He don't know some fellow done said the same thing about catching somebody around Betty Jean. That fellow . . . he go over to see Betty Sue while this other fellow sniffing around his Betty Jean. Sooner or later . . . somebody gonna get their wires crossed. Somebody gonna see Betty Jean when he should have been seeing Betty Sue and that'll be all she wrote for him. The only thing left to do is write it on his tombstone. "Here lie Bubba Boo. Was caught with Betty Jean instead of Betty Sue."

DOUB

They got that on a whole lot of tombstones.
            (*The phone rings.* FIELDING *answers it.*)

FIELDING

Car service. (*pause*) Yeah, sure I'll tell him. Turnbo, that was Aunt Lil. She say you supposed to pick her up at the doctors.

TURNBO (*exasperated*)

You know she done joined the Jehovah Witness. When I come back I'll be able to tell you anything you wanna know about the Bible.

(TURNBO *exits. The phone rings.*)

FIELDING

Car service. (*pause*) Yeah, I'll be right there. Green car.

DOUB

No, wait a minute. I thought Becker put you out.

FIELDING

Aw, me and Becker straight.
(FIELDING *exits.* YOUNGBLOOD *enters carrying tools.*)

YOUNGBLOOD

I cleancd the flywheel and replaced the belt. Another ten thousand miles and you gonna need a new alternator.

DOUB

Thanks.

YOUNGBLOOD

Hey, Doub, what's this I hear about the station closing?

DOUB

You just now finding out? They fixing to board up the whole block. Tear it down and build some houses.

YOUNGBLOOD

Damn! What they wanna do that for?

DOUB

I'm glad to see them do it. It's about time they done some-thing around here. They been talking for years about how they was gonna fix it up.

YOUNGBLOOD

White folks ain't got no sense of timing. They wait till I get in the position to buy me a house and then they pull the rug out from under me!

DOUB

That white man ain't paying you no mind. You ought to stop thinking like that. They been planning to tear these shacks down before you was born. You keep thinking everybody's against you and you ain't never gonna get nothing. I seen a hundred niggers too lazy to get up out the bed in the morning, talking about the white man is against them. That's just an excuse. You want to make something of your life, then the opportunity is there. You just have to shake off that "White folks is against me" attitude. Hell, they don't even know you alive.

YOUNGBLOOD

They knew I was alive when they drafted me and sent me over to Vietnam to be shot at. They knew I was alive then!

DOUB

You ain't the only one they sent. They sent a whole lot of other folks too. Some of them wasn't lucky enough to make it back alive. You ain't the only one been in the army. I went into the army in nineteen fifty. Looking to make something of myself. That was after the war. I didn't know they was gonna pull out a map, stick a pin in it and say "Let's go kill some people over here." I wasn't in the army but four months and they had me in Korea. Second Division. Company B. Fourth Battalion. It was a detail company. I think at that time the only dead body I had seen was my grandmama when Foster buried her. That's all I knew about a dead body. But I was meant to find out quick. The third day they put us on some trucks and drove out to the front lines. I was scared as I could get. The last words I remember my mama saying to me was how she was praying I didn't get sent to the front lines. I wasn't in Korea but three days and here I was on the front lines. Got out there and everything was quiet. The sergeant told us to get down off the trucks. We got down and started walking. Got near about two hundred yards when we saw our first body. Then another one. Then three more. The sergeants say "All right boys, we gonna clean up. I want you to stack the bodies six high." I never will forget that. "I want you to stack the bodies six high." Not five. Not seven. Six high. And that's what I did for the next nine months. Clean up the battlefield. It took me six months before I got to where I could keep my supper down. After that it didn't bother me no more. Never did learn how to do nothing else. They was supposed to teach me but they never did. They just never paid me no mind. There was a whole bunch of us they never paid no mind. What I'm trying to tell you is the white man ain't got no personal war against you cause you buying a house and they gonna tear down this block. You too young to be depending on driving jitneys. Is that what you want to do all your life?

YOUNGBLOOD

Naw, but where else am I gonna make fifty dollars a day tax free? Where else am I gonna get the advantage of not paying taxes?

DOUB

How old are you? Twenty-four? Why don't you go to school under the G.I. Bill? Become something. Make something of your life. You can be anything you want. Be a pilot or a engineer or something. Like I tell my boys, the world's opened up to you. When I was your age, the only thing you could get a job doing was busing dishes, running elevators and cleaning out toilets. Things like that. It ain't like that now. You can be anything you want. You're young, act kinda crazy, but you got some sense. You don't waste your money. You got sense enough to buy a house. Go on to school, Youngblood. You too young to be counting on driving jitneys.

YOUNGBLOOD

I'm worried about right now. How I'm gonna get me some furniture and pay that three hundred dollar a month mortgage.

DOUB

Why don't you try to get on with another station.

YOUNGBLOOD

They all filled up. If Ace hadn't died I wouldn't even have got on here.

DOUB

Talk to Becker. See if he can get you on down at the mill. He got some pull down there.

YOUNGBLOOD

I don't want to work in no mill. I done seen what the mills do to people and I swore I'd never work in no mill. The mills suck all the life out of you. That's not for me. I don't want that. I'll do anything but I don't want that.

(The phone rings. DOUB *goes to answer it.)*

DOUB

It ain't all the time what you want. Sometime it's what you need. Black folks always get the two confused. (*into phone*) Car service. (*pause*) Naw, he ain't here right now. I'll tell him.
    (*He hangs up the phone.*)
Somebody named Glucker from J & L Steel wants Becker to call him back.

YOUNGBLOOD

Hey Doub, what you gonna do when the station close?

DOUB

I don't know. Becker talking about quitting. I wanted to get together and see if we can find a place to move the station. If that don't work, I guess I'll just run the bus line till something else comes up. I ain't too worried. I got my railroad pension, and I ain't got nobody but myself, so I'll be all right.
    (*FIELDING enters.*)

FIELDING

Hey, Doub. Youngblood. We ain't got but two more weeks, huh?

DOUB

Yeah, that's right. They gonna board it up first of the month.

FIELDING

What you gonna do?

DOUB

I don't know, Fielding.

FIELDING

Well, it's a shame. That's all I got to say about it. You see Becker's boy yesterday?

DOUB

Naw, I ain't seen him. Did he come by here?

FIELDING

Oh, yeah, he come by. Me and Turnbo was here. Good-looking boy. He come by to see his daddy. Big, strong boy. Youngblood, you and Turnbo get straightened out?

YOUNGBLOOD
We okay. As long as he stay out my business.

FIELDING
You all ain't gonna be okay long. Turnbo's just like that.
He get in everybody's business. You can't pay him no
mind. You got to ignore what he say.

DOUB
What . . . you and Turnbo had some words?

FIELDING
Turnbo pulled a gun on him.

DOUB
He did what?

FIELDING
Pulled a gun on him.

DOUB
That nigger's crazy. He's gonna kill somebody one of these
days with that damn gun. Either that or somebody's gonna
kill him. That makes the fourth or fifth time he done pulled
that gun on somebody. One time he pulled that gun on a man
for fifty cents. Man took a trip and told him he'd pay him
later. Turnbo seen the man sitting next door eating breakfast.
He went in there . . . kicked open the door . . . waving that
gun around. Talking about killing somebody over fifty cents.
The man ain't had a penny. He done talked the waitress into
letting him owe her too, and Turnbo wanna go in there and
shoot the man. Somebody had to give him fifty cents to keep
him from getting killed. You mark my words. One of these
times he's gonna end up killing somebody.
    (TURNBO enters and everyone falls silent as they
    look at him.)

TURNBO
You all want me to go back out so you can finish.

DOUB
I don't care what you do.

TURNBO
You all got quiet . . . like you was talking about me.

FIELDING

Naw, we wasn't . . .

DOUB

Yeah, we was talking about you. We was talking about how you gonna pull that gun on the wrong person one of these days.

TURNBO

You ain't got nothing to do with that, Doub. I ain't gonna let nobody take advantage of me, that's all, and that boy ain't got but one more time.

DOUB

Yeah, you right. I ain't got nothing to do with it. Let me shut up.
(DOUB *crosses to the door.*)
Youngblood, if you see Becker don't forget to tell him that Glucker from the mill called.
(DOUB *exits.*)

FIELDING

Somebody called Becker from the mill?

TURNBO

Must be about Shealy's nephew. That boy broke into Taylor's with old man Pitt's son. Becker's trying to get him a job at the mill.

FIELDING

Oh, well he can do that. He's got a lot of pull down there. He done got a whole lot of people jobs. What you gonna do Turnbo when the station close down?

TURNBO

Oh, I'm set. I talked to Lewellen down on Centre. I'm gonna take Jim Bono's place. Bono's in the hospital with cancer.

FIELDING

No kidding. That's a shame.

TURNBO

What you gonna do?

FIELDING

I don't know. Doub say something about finding another place. I'm gonna wait and see what Becker say.

TURNBO

What about you, Youngblood?

YOUNGBLOOD

I ain't got nothing to say to you.

TURNBO

If that's the way you want it.

YOUNGBLOOD

You just stay clear of me, old man. Next time you gonna get hurt for real.

TURNBO

I ain't gonna let nobody do nothing to me.

FIELDING

Don't you all start now. Come on and be friends.

TURNBO

I ain't started nothing. I tried to talk to the man, willing to let bygones be bygones and he wanna threaten me.
    (The phone rings.)

YOUNGBLOOD

I done said all I got to say to you.

TURNBO

Well all right then. If that's the way you want it. Good!
    (TURNBO goes to answer the phone.)
Car service. *(pause)* Fielding.
    (He hands him the phone.)

FIELDING

Hello? Oh, hi, Miss Mayberry. *(pause)* Sure, I'll take you shopping. Are you ready now? *(pause)* I'll be right there.
    (FIELDING bumps into SHEALY as he exits.
    SHEALY enters. He is dressed up.)

SHEALY

Did I get any calls this morning?

YOUNGBLOOD

Not that I know.

SHEALY

That gal say she was gonna call me at ten o'clock. I knew she was lying when she said it. Becker been here yet?

TURNBO

I ain't seen him. I hear Becker's upset about you using the phone to take numbers.

SHEALY

Becker's always upset about something.
(*The phone rings, and* TURNBO *goes to answer it.* BOOSTER *enters.*)

TURNBO

(*into phone*) Car service. Shealy.
(TURNBO *hands the phone to* SHEALY.)

BOOSTER

Hey fellows. My old man been around here?

TURNBO

I ain't seen him all day. I just got here though. Youngblood, Becker been by at all?

YOUNGBLOOD

I ain't seen him.

SHEALY (*into phone*)

Yeah. Three forty-seven . . .

TURNBO

He should be back in a minute.

SHEALY

. . . and six seventeen boxed for fifty cents . . . nine twenty-nine straight for a dollar.
(*He takes out his pad and writes.*)
Yeah. Okay.
(*He hangs up the phone.*)

BOOSTER

You take numbers?

TURNBO

Yeah. Shealy, this is Becker's son. That's Shealy. He the
number man.

BOOSTER

Give me three dollars on three nineteen, straight.
(SHEALY *writes the number and gives* BOOSTER
his slip.)

BOOSTER

If you all see my old man, tell him I was by to see him.
(BOOSTER *exits.*)

YOUNGBLOOD

Shealy, I'm going next door to clean up. If Becker comes,
tell him I got a message for him.

SHEALY

I ain't gonna be hanging around here all day. I'm gonna
give that gal five more minutes.

TURNBO

Go on, I'll tell him.

YOUNGBLOOD

That's all right, I'll be right back.
(YOUNGBLOOD *exits.*)

TURNBO

That boy ain't got good sense.

SHEALY

I hear you all had a go at it.

TURNBO

He's a damn fool.
(*The phone rings.* TURNBO *answers it.*)
(*into phone*) Car service. (*pause*) Shealy.

SHEALY

Shealy. (*pause*) Hey baby! (*pause*) Sure. That's what I told
you. Where you at? (*pause*) Don't move. Stay right there.
I'll be there in five minutes.
(*He hangs up the phone.*)
Come on, Turnbo. Give me a ride down to the Ellis Hotel.

This might be the one! If I don't see Rosie's face, I'll give you five dollars for the trip!

(The phone rings.)

*(*TURNBO *and* SHEALY *exit. Presently,* YOUNGBLOOD *enters carrying a cup of coffee. He takes out his book and begins to figure in it.* RENA *enters.)*

YOUNGBLOOD

What you want around here?

RENA

I want to see you. You didn't come home last night.

YOUNGBLOOD

That's right. What for? You tell me, huh? What I'm gonna come home for? Being as how you might not be there.

RENA

Where did you go?

YOUNGBLOOD

What you care about where I went? I stayed here, if you got to know. I slept on the couch. What I'm gonna come home for with you making all them stupid accusations?

RENA

I ain't made no accusations. I just said I knew about you and Peaches.

YOUNGBLOOD

Somebody tell you they seen your sister in my car and you jump to conclusions. You don't know what I'm doing.

RENA

You right. I don't know what you doing. That's what I'm saying. It ain't like you ain't got no track record. If I remember correctly, you was leading the parade.

YOUNGBLOOD

I'm here. That should be enough. If I didn't want to be here I'd be somewhere else. Why can't you just take that?

RENA

Because it's not enough. I don't want somebody that think just cause they there, that's enough . . . they don't have to do nothing else. I want somebody who's gonna share with me . . . not hide things from me.

YOUNGBLOOD

You want to know what I was hiding from you? I'll tell you. I been hustling . . . working day and night . . . while you accuse me of running the streets . . . and all I'm trying to do is save enough money so I can buy a house so you and Jesse have someplace decent to live. I asked Peaches if she would go with me to look at houses, cause I wanted to surprise you. I wanted to pull a truck up to the house and say, "Come on, baby, we moving." And drive on out to Penn Hills and pull that truck up in front of one of them houses and say, "This is yours. This is your house baby." That's what she was trying to hide from you. That's why Turnbo seen her riding in my car all the time. I found a house and I come up a hundred and fifty dollars short from closing the deal, and I come and took the eighty dollars out the drawer.

RENA

A house? A house, Darnell? You bought a house without me!

YOUNGBLOOD

I wanted to surprise you.

RENA

You gonna surprise me with a house? Don't do that. A new TV maybe. A stereo . . . a couch . . . a refrigerator . . . okay. But don't surprise me with a house that I didn't even have a chance to pick out! That's what you been doing? That's the debt you had to pay?

YOUNGBLOOD

You always saying you don't want to live your whole life in the projects.

RENA

Darnell, you ain't bought no house without me. How many times in your life do you get to pick out a house?

YOUNGBLOOD

Wait till you see it. It's real nice. It's all on one floor . . . it's got a basement . . . like a little den. We can put the TV down there. I told myself Rena's gonna like this. Wait till she see I bought her a house.

RENA

Naw, you bought a den for Darnell . . . that's what you did.
So you can sit down there and watch your football games.
But what about the kitchen? The bathroom? How many win-
dows does it have in the bedroom? Is there some place for
Jesse to play? How much closet space does it have? You
can't just surprise me with a house and I'm supposed to say,
"Oh, Darnell, that's nice." At one time I would have. But I'm
not seventeen no more. I have responsibilities. I want to
know if it has a hookup for a washer and dryer cause I got
to wash Jesse's clothes. I want to know if it has a yard and
do it have a fence and how far Jesse has to go to school. I
ain't thinking about where to put the TV. That's not what's
important to me. And you supposed to know, Darnell. You
supposed to know what's important to me like I'm supposed
to know what's important to you. I'm not asking you to do it
by yourself. I'm here with you. We in this together. See . . .
house or no house we still ain't got the food money. But if
you had come and told me . . . if you had shared that with me
. . . we could have went to my mother and we could have got
eighty dollars for the house and still had money for food.
You just did it all wrong, Darnell. I mean, you did the right
thing but you did it wrong.

YOUNGBLOOD

No matter what I do it's gonna come out wrong with you.
That's why you jump to conclusions. That's why you
accused me of running around with Peaches.

You can't look and see that I quit going to parties all the
time . . . that I quit running with Ba Bra and Earl . . . that
I quit chasing women. You just look at me and see the old
Darnell. If you can't change the way you look at me . . .
then I may as well surrender now. I can't beat your memory of who I was if you can't see I've changed. I go out
here and work like a dog to try and do something nice for
you and no matter what I do, I can't never do it right cause
all you see is the way I used to be. You don't see the new
Darnell. You don't see I've changed.

RENA

I know people change . . . but I know they can slip back too.

YOUNGBLOOD

No, Rena . . . people believe what they want to believe . . .
what they set up in their mind to believe. I know what it
looked like when I was gone all the time and not bringing
home any money. But you could have noticed that I was tired
. . . you could have said, "Darnell ain't talking too much cause
he's tired." You could have noticed that I didn't act like somebody running the streets . . . that I didn't come home smelling
like alcohol and perfume . . . that I didn't dress like somebody
running the streets. If you had thought it all the way through,
you could have noticed how excited I was when I got the UPS
job . . . how I asked you if I could take it . . . you would have
noticed how I was planning things . . . that I wasn't sitting
around drinking beer and playing cards . . . how I would get
up early on Sunday and go out to the airport to try to make a
few extra dollars before the jitney station opened. But you
ain't seen all that. You ain't seen the new Darnell. You still
working off your memory. But the past is over and done with.
I'm thinking about the future. You not the only one who thinks
about Jesse. That's why I'm trying to do something different.
That's why I'm trying to buy a house. Maybe I should have
told you about the house. Maybe I did do it wrong. But I done
it.   I   tried   to   show   you
I loved you, but what I get for it?

RENA

Okay, Darnell . . . you right. I could have seen all that. But
what you ain't looking at is I changed too. We are both different people than we were . . . than when we first fell in
love. I still love you, Darnell. But love can only go so far.
When we were in high school that was enough. That was
the world. That was everything. But it ain't everything no
more. I don't have all the answers . . . sometimes I don't
even have the right questions, but I do know it takes two
to find them. All I know is we got somebody, a little two-
year-old boy, counting on us.

YOUNGBLOOD

But I know when you place your hand in mine you got to
say, "Darnell's not gonna let me down . . . he loves me." I
don't want to make no more mistakes in life. I don't want
to do nothing to mess this up. I don't want to get old and
be talking about I had me this little old gal one time . . . but

I ain't seen her in twenty-two years.

RENA

If that's not what you want then you got to let me know,
Darnell. If we don't know what's important to one another
and learn to share that then we can't make it. We can't
make it with each other.

YOUNGBLOOD

I want you baby . . . I told you that. You already my pride.
I want you to be my joy. Cause there ain't but one thing I
done wrong . . . stay away from you one night too long.
    (They kiss for a long moment.)

RENA

Where's this house at?

YOUNGBLOOD

Penn Hills. It's got a nice kitchen too. Got a little yard. Got
a nice bedroom. Got a real nice bedroom.

RENA

Oh, yeah. I can't wait to see it.

YOUNGBLOOD

Where's my boy?

RENA

At my mother's house. I got to go to my accounting class.

YOUNGBLOOD

You wanna ride?

RENA

I'll walk. I need the exercise.

YOUNGBLOOD

Naw I'll give you a ride. I don't want to let you out of my
sight. Matter of fact you might have to miss that accounting class.

RENA

What? You got something to teach me?
    (They kiss again as BECKER *enters.)*

BECKER

Hey . . . Hey . . . You all got to take that home.

RENA

How you doing, Mr. Becker?

BECKER

Oh, I'm all right. How you all doing?

YOUNGBLOOD

Well, Becker . . . I done bought me a house.

BECKER

Oh, yeah. Where'd you buy it at?

YOUNGBLOOD

Penn Hills.

BECKER

Good! They got some nice houses out there. That's a smart move, Youngblood. I'm glad to see you do it. Ain't nothing like owning some property. They might even call you for jury duty. Most young men be on the other side of the law. How old is the baby now?

RENA

Two. He look like he's three. Big as he is.

BECKER

Ain't nothing left to do now but to get married. Come November it'll be seventeen years that me and Lucille been together. Seventeen years. I told her say, "Work with me." She say okay. I wasn't sure what it meant myself. I thought it meant pull or push together. But she showed me one can push and the other can pull . . . as long as it's in the same direction. You know what I mean? It ain't all gonna flow together all the time. That's life. As long as it don't break apart. When you look around you'll see that all you got is each other. There ain't much more. Even when it look like there is . . . you come one day to find out there ain't much more worth having. Now I ain't getting in your business or nothing Youngblood, but the next time you feel like you want to spend the night apart . . . do like I do . . . go sleep on the couch in the living room. Don't put your business in the street. You put your business in the street you'd be surprised how many people wanna have a hand in it.

                    YOUNGBLOOD

I found that out. Even if it ain't in the street people wanna put it there.

                    BECKER

See you're learning. Soon you gonna know as much as I do. You and Turnbo getting along all right? He been in here?

                    YOUNGBLOOD

Yeah. We all right. Some man from J & L called here for you. He wants you to call him back. Name of Glucker, I think. Something like that.

                    BECKER

If you see Doub or Turnbo or Fielding, tell them we gonna have a meeting tonight at seven o'clock. See what we can do about them boarding up the place.

                    YOUNGBLOOD

Okay, I'll tell them. Come on, baby, before you be late for class.
        *(*YOUNGBLOOD *and* RENA *exit.* BECKER *crosses to
        the phone and dials.)*

                    BECKER *(into phone)*

Mr. Glucker in Personnel. *(pause)* Jim Becker. *(pause)* Mr. Glucker? Becker here. *(pause)* When? *(pause)* Sure I'll be glad to do it for you. *(pause)* All right. That's no problem. You can count on me. Say, Glucker, I got a young man that's trying to do something with his life, trying to straighten himself out. I wanna send him over to see you. *(pause)* Well, that'll help. Even something temporary let him show you what kind of worker he is. Thanks. I'll send him over to see you. His name is Robert Shealy. All right now. Thanks again.
        *(*BECKER *hangs up the phone and busies himself
        with straightening up the station.* BOOSTER *enters.)*
The station's closed. Ain't no cars here. You might go up on Webster, corner of Roberts. Maceo Brown got a station up there.

                    BOOSTER

I been thinking about what you said. So many things to

think about. After twenty years I thought I got good at thinking . . . but there's so many things you miss. I went out and visited Mama's grave . . .

(BECKER *ignores* BOOSTER. *He gathers up his papers and things and exits the station.* BOOSTER *is stunned. He gathers himself together and starts to exit when* FIELDING *enters.*)

FIELDING

I just saw your daddy. He must have went on a trip. How you doing?

BOOSTER

Fine. I'm doing fine. Just trying to figure out what to do.

FIELDING

If you in the treetop you can't do nothing but jump to the ground. But first you got to know how you got up there. Did you climb up to get some apples or was you run up by a bear? You got to know that cause you might have to start running when you hit the ground. If you trying to figure out what to do . . . you got to first figure out how you got in the situation you in. That's something simple. But you be surprised how many people can't figure that out.

(FIELDING *looks at* BOOSTER's *suit.*)

Is that what they give you? They ought to be ashamed of themselves. That cheap-ass wool ain't but a dollar ninety-nine cents a yard. They could have give you a nice wool gabardine. A good-looking young man like you . . . they could look at you and tell you a connoisseur of fine haberdashery.

(FIELDING *looks at the suit again with the experienced eye of a tailor.*)

I could open up them armpits . . . add some new shoulder-pads . . . move them buttons . . . lay a double-cross top stitch on that lapel . . . everybody don't know that double-cross top stitch. Ain't but so many fellows can make a double-cross top stitch. At one time in the whole city of Pittsburgh there wasn't but two. Me and Jimmy Green. And he couldn't make it but so good.

BOOSTER

I see you know something about it.

FIELDING

I used to make suits for Billy Ekstine. I used to make all his clothes. He wouldn't let nobody else make them. He get out there on the road and them fellows in the bands be jealous of him. They used to try and outdo each other you know. Used to try and keep the name of their tailors secret. Count Basie found out I was Billy Ekstine's tailor . . . come through here and wouldn't leave till I had made him a suit. Fucked up his whole tour. Had to cancel Cleveland and Cincinnati while he waited them ten days for that suit. Cost him twenty thousand dollars in lost revenue but he say he didn't care. He tried to steal me away from Billy, but Billy was from Pittsburgh and that made us have more of a bond. Even though I must say I liked Basie cause he paid well. But that wasn't enough to tear me and Billy apart.

(He pulls out his bottle and takes a drink.)

The only thing that could do that was this here bottle. That tore a whole lot of things apart. It don't always turn out like you think it is. You don't always have the kind of life that you dream about. You know what I mean?

BOOSTER

I thought I was gonna be the heavyweight champion of the world. Be the next Albert Einstein. But I forgot you can't live in your dreams. I found that out when I was seven. I dreamt I had a bicycle. I went all over on the bicycle. I rode it around in circles. I rode it everywhere.

I rode it to the store. I rode it to school. I went all over on the bicycle. Red bicycle. Had a coonskin tail hanging from the handlebars. Had a little bell on the handlebars. Anybody get in your way you just ring that. Had real nice reflectors. Big old seat seem like it too big for you, but then again it seem like it was just big enough. Had fenders in the back . . . a little seat back there in case you want to give somebody a ride they could sit back there. That was one of the nicest bicycles anybody ever wanna see. I woke up and went looking for it. I had to go to school. Where the bike? Why don't I just hop on that? I looked all over for it. I looked in the back yard. The neighbor's yard. Where the bicycle? That's when I decided right then that dreams didn't mean anything in this world. You could be the president or a bishop or something like that. You can dream you got more money than Rockefeller. See what happen when you wake up.

FIELDING

You can dream lucky and wake up cold in hand. That's what my daddy used to say.
(FIELDING *drinks from the bottle.*)
I ain't supposed to do this. I can't let Becker catch me. That's against Becker's rules. I guess you know something about that, huh?

BOOSTER

Something about what?

FIELDING

I say you must know something about Becker's rules.

BOOSTER

Yeah, I guess I do. Becker's rules is what got me in the penitentiary.

FIELDING

I ain't gonna carry it that far.
(FIELDING *takes a drink and offers the bottle to* BOOSTER, *who takes a swig and hands the bottle back to* FIELDING. *He crosses to the door.*)

BOOSTER

I'll see you around.
(BOOSTER *exits.* FIELDING *takes another nip.* PHILMORE *enters. He carries a duffle-bag. He looks closely at* FIELDING.)

PHILMORE

Do I know you?

FIELDING

I know you. I know you live out in Homewood above the Frankstown Bar cause I done carried you out there a couple times.

PHILMORE

I used to live out there. My old lady put me out. She don't know but she gonna be missing me. Come next week she gonna be begging me to come back. You watch.

FIELDING

I don't doubt it.

PHILMORE

I went to my sister but she wouldn't let me stay there. Now I got to go to my mama's.

FIELDING

Mama will take you in.

PHILMORE

How much you charge to go out to East Liberty?

FIELDING

That cost three dollars.

PHILMORE

Look here I ain't got but two dollars. Carry me out there I'll give it to you. I work down there at the William Penn Hotel. I been working down there six years. Never missed a day. Let me owe you a dollar. I'll give it to you next week.

FIELDING

All right. Come on.

PHILMORE

Mama don't like to see you coming . . . but she will take you in.

FIELDING

You got to have somebody you can count on. Now you take my wife. I ain't seen that woman in twenty-two years. I had a dream once . . .

(FIELDING *and* PHILMORE *exit as phone rings. Lights go down on the scene.*)

SCENE 2

(The lights come up on the scene. It is early evening. TURNBO, FIELDING, YOUNGBLOOD, *and* DOUB *sit in a circle listening to* BECKER. *The lights and postures of the men convey the idea of a clandestine meeting.)*

BECKER

All right . . . you all know why we're here. You all know what's happening. The city's fixing to board up the place come the first of the month. They gonna tear it down. They gonna tear the whole block down.

YOUNGBLOOD

They gonna tear the whole neighborhood down.

DOUB

They supposed to build some houses. That's what they need to do.

TURNBO

They supposed to build a new hospital down there on Logan Street. They been talking about that for the longest while. They supposed to build another part to the Irene Kaufman Settlement House to replace the part they tore down. They supposed to build some houses down on Dinwidee.

BECKER

Turnbo's right. They *supposed* to build some houses but you ain't gonna see that. You ain't gonna see nothing but the tear-down. That's all I ever seen.

YOUNGBLOOD

That's all there is to see.

FIELDING

They built that Senior Citizen highrise on Bedford.

YOUNGBLOOD

We ain't talking about no one building. We talking about the neighborhood.

BECKER

All right. Since they boarding up the place we got to figure out what we gonna do. I talked to Tanenhill about renting that place down on Centre what used to be Siegal's egg store. We can do that. Or we can try to get on with another station. We can go on and play by their rules like we have been. When I first come along I tried to do everything right. I figured that was the best thing to do. Even when it didn't look like they was playing fair I told myself they would come around. Time it look like you got a little something going for you they would change the rules. Now you got to do something else. I told myself that's all right my boy's coming. He's gonna straighten it out. I put it on somebody else. I took it off of me and put it on somebody else. I told myself as long as I could do that then I could just keep going along and making excuses for everybody. But I'm through making excuses for anybody . . . including myself. I ain't gonna pass it on. I say we stay here. We already here. The people know we here. We been here for eighteen years . . . and I don't see no reason to move. City or no city. I look around and all I see is boarded up buildings. Some of them been boarded-up for more than ten years. If they want to build some houses that's when they can tear it down. When they ready to build the houses. They board this place up the first of the month and let it sit boarded-up for the next fifteen . . . twenty years.

TURNBO

That's just how they put Memphis Lee out of business.

BECKER

And if we don't do something they'll put Clifford out of business. Put Hester out of business. Put us out of business. Let Clifford go on and sell his fish sandwich till they get ready to build something. Let Hester go on and sell her milk and butter. Cause we gonna run jitneys out of here till the day before the bulldozer come! Ain't gonna be no boarding up around here! *(the men give cries of approval)* We gonna fight them on that. Let them go board up somewhere else.

FIELDING

Sounds good to me.

TURNBO

Come to think of it . . . what they gonna do about it? If we
say no we ain't moving. What they gonna do about it?

FIELDING

If everybody stick together they can't do nothing.

BECKER

We gonna have to raise the dues ten dollars a month . . .

YOUNGBLOOD

Why?

BECKER

To help pay our legal fees. We gonna get us a lawyer. We
going in with Clifford and Hester and get us a lawyer. Do it
legal. There's ways to fight them. If we gonna be running jitneys out of here we gonna do it right. We get us a lawyer he
can go down to the court and file a petition. Now there's a
couple things that come up we need to take care of. I want all
the cars inspected. The people got a right if you hauling them
around in your car to expect the brakes to work. Clean out
your trunk. Clean out the interior of your car. Keep your car
clean. The people want to ride in a clean car. We providing a
service to the community. We ain't just giving rides to people.
We providing a service. That's why you answer the phone
"Car service." You don't say Becker's Cabs or Joe's Jitney's.
Part of that service is providing people with a way to get
their groceries home or to get their suitcase down to the bus
station or the airport so they can go home to visit their
mama or whoever it is they want to visit. I want everybody
to pull their weight and provide the service that's expected
of us. (BECKER *looks at his watch*) Time getting away. I got
to go down and work at J & L . . . they got caught short-
handed and need somebody who knows how to operate
them machines . . . I'll be over there every night this week.
But remember . . . come next week . . . come Tuesday . . .
ain't no plywood going up around here. Ain't gonna be no
boarding up this station! Youngblood . . .
(*He takes a dollar out of his pocket.*)
Run over Hester's and get us a light bulb for that lamp.
(YOUNGBLOOD *exits.*)

DOUB

Hey Becker, what lawyer we gonna get?

BECKER

I don't know, Doub. I ain't thought too much about it.

TURNBO

We ought to get Wendell Freeman. He the one who won that suit for the NAACP when they wouldn't let no colored in them houses out there in Shadyside. As much money as he made on that . . . he ought to work for free.

FIELDING

How you figure he ought to work for free? Who you know work for free? Go ahead . . . name anybody. Who you know work for free?

TURNBO

I wasn't talking to you, Fielding.

DOUB

Whoever it is ought to be on our side. Half the time they be worried about what the city gonna say or think about them. I seen that happen.

BECKER

Yeah, I have too. You can bet whoever we get gonna be on our side. We ain't going through all of this for nothing. Let me get on over to the mill before the shift start. Say Doub . . . oh, never mind. I'll see you tomorrow.

(BECKER *exits.*)

TURNBO

I'm going over and see what Clifford has to say about them boarding up his place.

DOUB

Here . . . I'll go over with you.

(*He crosses to the door.*)

You coming Fielding?

(FIELDING *indicates a lack of interest.*)

Come on, I'll buy you a fish sandwich.

FIELDING

Oh yeah . . . since you put it like that. (DOUB *and* TURBO *exit.* FIELDING *takes a bottle of whiskey from his pocket and starts to take a drink, then changes his mind.*) A little lemonade never killed nobody.

(FIELDING *exits. The lights go down on the scene.*)

SCENE 3

(The lights come up on the station the following day. DOUB *and* TURNBO *sit in chairs.* FIELDING *leans against the wall by the phone. Everyone is silent and in a solemn mood. The silence swells.* FIELDING *breaks the silence.)*

FIELDING
Becker was all right by me. We had our run-ins and all, but he was all right by me.
(The phone rings. FIELDING *answers it.)*
Hello? *(pause)* Yeah.*(pause)* All right. Be right there.
(He hangs up the phone.)
I got a trip.
*(*FIELDING *exits.)*

TURNBO
When is the funeral, you know?

DOUB
It ain't been set yet.

TURNBO
I wonder if he had any insurance.

DOUB
What you care whether the man had any insurance!

TURNBO
I was just wondering. I'm allowed to wonder. I got some-thing on my mind I just say it. Ain't nothing wrong . . .

DOUB
Turnbo, shut up!

TURNBO

Ain't no sense in me staying here and trying to talk to a damn fool!

> (TURNBO *gets up and exits.* DOUB *sits staring at the wall. The phone rings.*)

DOUB (*into phone*)

Ain't no cars here today.

> (*He hangs up the phone as* YOUNGBLOOD *enters.*)

YOUNGBLOOD

Hey, Doub.

DOUB

Youngblood.

YOUNGBLOOD

Where's everybody?

DOUB

Fielding went on a trip.

YOUNGBLOOD

I seen Turnbo out there sitting in his car.

DOUB

He was in here running off at the mouth.

> (YOUNGBLOOD *and* DOUB *sit for a moment in silence.*)

YOUNGBLOOD

You couldn't find a nicer man than Becker. You know? Always keeping things straight. Always worried about somebody else. Always looking out for you.

DOUB

Yeah.

> (SHEALY *enters.*)

SHEALY

Hey, Doub. Youngblood.

DOUB

You heard?

SHEALY

Yeah, I heard it on the news last night. Man work all them years down there and ain't nothing happened. Retire . . . and go back to work one day . . . and that's the day the bolt decides to break. I can't understand it. It don't make no sense to me. I went to see Lucille and take her some money. She hit for a quarter a couple of days ago.

DOUB

How's she taking it?

SHEALY

She's taking it pretty good. Considering how it happened. Sudden and all.

DOUB

I'll have to get by and see her.
        (PHILMORE *enters. He is sober and somber.*)

SHEALY

Hey, Philmore.

PHILMORE

I'm sorry about Mr. Becker. I heard he got killed in an accident down at the mill. He was a nice man.

DOUB

Yeah. Thanks.

PHILMORE

You all need any pall-bearers?

DOUB

As soon as the arrangements are made, I will let you know. Don't nobody know too much right now.

PHILMORE

If you do . . . let me know. I'll take off work.
        (DOUB *shakes* PHILMORE*'s hand.*)

DOUB

Thanks Philmore. Thanks for coming around.
        (PHILMORE *exits.* SHEALY *goes into his pocket.*)

SHEALY

Here go ten dollars for flowers.

DOUB

All right.

YOUNGBLOOD

Here's mine.

SHEALY

You know that boy hit for three dollars yesterday.

DOUB

Who?

SHEALY

Becker's boy. Hit on that three nineteen.

DOUB

Anybody seen him?

SHEALY

Lucille say she ain't heard from him.

DOUB

I wonder do he know?
    (FIELDING *enters.*)

FIELDING

Hey, Shealy.

DOUB

We taking ten dollars for flowers, Fielding.
    (FIELDING *goes into his pocket and counts out
    eight dollars to* DOUB.*)

FIELDING

Loan me two dollars, Youngblood.

DOUB

Here, I'll put it with the four dollars you owe me.
    (TURNBO *enters.*)

FIELDING

What four dollars I owe you?

TURNBO

You know you borrowed four dollars off the man the other day. See, Doub, that's why I wouldn't loan him nothing.

FIELDING

I don't know nothing about no four dollars.

DOUB

That's all right, goddamn it! I know! You just give me six back. Give me ten dollars Turnbo.

TURNBO

Ten dollars for what?

DOUB

For flowers. Everybody's putting in ten dollars.

FIELDING

How the hell you figure I owe you six dollars?

DOUB

I ain't studying you.

TURNBO

Oh, all right. Did Youngblood give you his?

DOUB

Nigger why don't you mind your business! For one time, huh?

FIELDING

Hey, Doub . . . what I got to give you six back for?

TURNBO

This is my business. I want to make sure everybody pay.

DOUB

Let me take care of that.

YOUNGBLOOD

You ain't got to worry about my business.

TURNBO

I ain't worried about your business. I just say . . .
(The door opens and BOOSTER *enters. Everybody falls silent.)*

BOOSTER

Hey fellas, my old man around?

(BOOSTER *notices something is wrong.*)

Hey, what's the matter?

(BOOSTER *notices everybody looking at him.*)

What you all sitting around looking at me for?

TURNBO

Ain't you heard?

BOOSTER

Heard what?

DOUB

Boy, don't you know your daddy's dead?

(*The phone rings.* BOOSTER *moves toward* DOUB.)

BOOSTER

Hey man! What you talking about? Huh? What you talking about?

(*He turns toward* FIELDING.)

What's he talking about my daddy dead?

(*He moves toward* DOUB.)

What you talking about man?

DOUB

He got killed down at the . . .

(BOOSTER *punches* DOUB *in the face.* YOUNG-
BLOOD, TURNBO, *and* SHEALY *grab* BOOSTER.)

BOOSTER

What you talking about nigger! (*They wrestle* BOOSTER *to
the ground.*) Let me go! Let me go! Let me go! That nigger tell me my daddy's dead! Let me go. That nigger tell
me my daddy's dead.

(*The lights go down to black.*)

SCENE 4

(The lights come up on the station. It is three days later. DOUB, YOUNGBLOOD, TURNBO, FIELDING, *and* SHEALY *sit around the station. They have just come back from the funeral.)*

DOUB
When you moving, Youngblood?

YOUNGBLOOD
Saturday.

SHEALY
I hear you bought a house in Penn Hills.

YOUNGBLOOD
Yeah.

SHEALY
They got some nice houses out there. Some of them boys play for the Steelers got houses out there. Them some nice houses.

TURNBO
They ain't as nice as the houses in Monroeville. Most people don't even buy houses in Penn Hills no more. They go out to Monroeville.

SHEALY
Let me see now . . . where you say your house was again? Which one did you buy? I keep forgetting.

YOUNGBLOOD
Reverend Flowers preached a pretty funeral.

FIELDING

Sure did. Made me want to join the church. Have somebody preach over me like that.

TURNBO

The only thing he can say about you is you an alcoholic.

FIELDING

I ain't studying you. Sure I drink. Everybody drink. You ought not to go around calling people names.

DOUB

Why don't you all hold up on that bickering back and forth. Don't nobody wanna hear that today.

SHEALY

You all still gonna stay here? You gonna fight them on boarding up the place, Doub?

TURNBO

What you worried for? The only thing is you won't have no place to take numbers. That's all you worried about.

SHEALY

I was talking to this man right here.

DOUB

I don't know, Shealy. It just wouldn't be the same without Becker.

FIELDING

Naw. Sure wouldn't.

YOUNGBLOOD

I'm ready if everybody else is. If not I'll find a job somewhere. Go to school. Raise my family. Do whatever I have to. You know.

FIELDING

Becker was all right by me. We had our run-ins. But he was all right by me.
    (*The door opens, and* BOOSTER *enters.*)

BOOSTER

I just wanted to stop by and thank you all for everything you done.

(He crosses to DOUB, *shakes his hand, and puts his arm around him.)*

DOUB

Sure. Ain't a man here wouldn't have done anything he could for Becker.

BOOSTER

Yeah, I know.

FIELDING

That's right. You can be proud of your daddy. He was all right by me. I ain't knowed him to have an enemy in the world. Ain't that right, Doub?

BOOSTER

I never knew him too much, you know. I never got to know him like you all did. I can't say nothing wrong by him. He took care of me when I was young. He ain't run the streets and fuss and fight with my mama. The only thing I ever knew him to do was work hard. It didn't matter to me too much at the time cause I couldn't see it like I see it now. He had his ways. I guess everybody do. The only thing I feel sorry about . . . is he ain't got out of life what he put in. He deserved better than what life gave him. I can't help thinking that. But you right . . . I'm proud of my old man. I'm proud of him. *(The phone rings.)* And I'm proud to be Becker's boy.

(He stops and catches himself.)

I didn't come here to preach no sermon.

(He starts toward the door. He stops and turns around. The phone continues to ring. He crosses to it and picks up the receiver.)

(into phone) Car service.

(The lights go down to black.)